TIME FOR
A
CHECKUP

TIME FOR A CHECKUP

EXAMINING OUR PROGRESS IN SPIRITUAL GROWTH

Alice R. Cullinan

CHRISTIAN • LITERATURE • CRUSADE
Fort Washington, Pennsylvania 19034

CHRISTIAN LITERATURE CRUSADE

U.S.A.
P.O. Box 1449, Fort Washington, PA 19034

GREAT BRITAIN
51 The Dean, Alresford, Hants., SO24 9BJ

AUSTRALIA
P.O. Box 91, Pennant Hills, N.S.W. 2120

NEW ZEALAND
P.O. Box 77, Ashhurst

©Alice R. Cullinan 1993
This Printing 1994

Cover photo:Superstock

ISBN 0-87508-739-6

In order to avoid spoiling your copy of this book, the charts on pages 19, 29, 39-40, 60-61, 81, 97, 114 and 126 may be photocopied for personal or group use FREE OF CHARGE.

PRINTED IN THE UNITED STATES OF AMERICA

In loving memory of my parents,

James M. Cullinan, Sr.,
and
Elizabeth B. Cullinan,

whose love and discipline made it easier for me to love and be obedient to my Heavenly Father.

TABLE OF CONTENTS

INTRODUCTION

Cathy, my niece, was so excited. She was sixteen now and had just received her driver's permit. For her birthday, her mother decided to purchase a used car that she could call her own. Being a single parent and a working mother, it had become difficult to chauffeur her to all the events at school and church. After visiting several used car lots, they found an old car that ran well but didn't look like much. In fact, Cathy requested that they not bring it home until after it had been painted. She didn't want any of her friends to see it parked in the driveway!

Cathy was given the privilege of selecting the color of paint for her "new car." None of us had any idea that she would select the most brilliant yellow we had ever seen. (Her family wasn't certain whether they wanted to park it in the driveway now!) But the proud sixteen-year-old was soon seen driving her yellow bomb everywhere in town, leaving a stream of smoke behind because of its age and condition.

Several months had passed when the phone rang one afternoon. "Alice," the trembling voice on the phone said, "could you pick me up? My car died." I sensed she wanted to say something else but was afraid to. "Cathy," I asked, "is anything wrong?" There was a moment of silence, and then a frightened reply. "I haven't been checking the oil like you and Mom told me to. Do you think the engine is burned up?"

Only a few weeks prior to this incident, one of her friends had ruined a car by letting it run out of oil. At that time, we strongly cautioned Cathy to be sure to keep the oil level checked in her car, since we knew it was using a great deal. We showed her where the dipstick was and told her how often to check it; we explained how and where to put in the oil if needed. We cautioned her that if she burned up the engine in this car, it would be a long time before she got another one.

Thankfully, that did not turn out to be the problem. She just needed an alternator. But the experience helped her to become more aware of the need for "regular checkups."

Several more months passed, and our church was having revival services. Cathy was especially convicted one evening concerning her own need for spiritual growth. After the service she shared with her mother and me some of her concerns and asked our advice on how she could tell if she was growing spiritually. We attempted to share with her some of the areas in our lives that should show evidence of spiritual growth and how to evaluate them for progress. I soon realized, however, that it was much easier to teach her how to read the "add oil" notch on the dipstick than to tell her how to evaluate her spiritual condition. It was out of this frustration that I began to try to formulate some specifics that would be helpful to her and to others in the matter of "checking up" on spiritual growth.

CHAPTER ONE

CHECKING UP ON YOUR BIBLE STUDY

Bible study is obviously one of the most important disciplines for the Christian if progress in spiritual growth is to occur. Unfortunately, many Christians seem to overlook the importance of a consistent, personal Bible study time, and therefore do not make much progress in this area of their lives. Apparently many Christians think spiritual growth can occur with little or no exposure to Bible study. Some seem to think that the Sunday School teacher's lessons and the preacher's sermons are sufficient for their spiritual diet. Many do not understand the importance of their own study of the Scriptures, or they simply do not know how to get anything out of reading it on their own. Still others fail to have a regular time or a systematic approach to the study of God's Word.

When I became a Christian, I was told how important Bible study is in the life of a growing Christian but was not given instruction or advice concerning ways to feed myself. I decided that I would try to read the Bible on my own. Because I was a baby Christian, however, I made the mistake of beginning in the book of Genesis and continuing straight on through the Old Testament—or attempting to! By the time I reached Leviticus, I was completely bogged down.

HOW IS YOUR PERSONAL BIBLE STUDY GOING?

It stands to reason that our spiritual lives need food for sustenance just as our physical lives do. Some of the rules we learned as children concerning our physical eating habits apply equally to the way we should eat spiritually.

1. We need to eat regularly. We would not think of eating only once or twice a week and expect to remain physically strong. We need to eat our spiritual food daily, also, in order for our spiritual lives to remain strong. Have you made Bible study a daily part of your life?

2. We need to eat slowly. If we bolt down our food, we will suffer the consequences. It also takes time to read the Bible and time to meditate on its truths if it is going to benefit us as it should. Do you have a time when you can read and think about various passages of the Bible without feeling the pressure of time or being interrupted by others?

3. We need a well-balanced diet. We often read of the effects of too much of this or too little of that in our diets. The same is true with the Word of God. A constant diet of prophecy without ever looking at the Law, for

instance, will be detrimental to our growth. Have you developed a plan for your Bible study that gives you opportunity to read various portions of God's Word?

4. We need an adequate supply of food. We can be eating well-balanced meals on a regular basis, allowing enough time, but if the quantity is not sufficient, we will be adversely affected. The same is true with the Word of God. Some of us read such a little amount of God's Word that it doesn't do us much good. It is not necessary to have several hours of free time available before we pick up the Bible, but it is necessary to read enough of it that God is able to speak to us a message for the day. How much of God's Word are you able to read meaningfully each day?

HAVE YOU CONSIDERED THE BENEFITS OF READING THE BIBLE?

It may be easy for you to be committed to reading the Bible because you have been convinced that a Christian should do so. But you may not be aware of the benefits. The Word of God itself mentions some of these benefits.

1. The Bible is a cleansing agent (Jn. 15:3). It is impossible for us to keep from getting contaminated by the world as we walk through each day. I remember one summer when I worked for a company where everyone in the office was an expert in using four-letter words. Being exposed to that language for eight hours a day left those words etched on my own mind.

I discovered one evening that if I read the Bible for about thirty minutes when I got home from work, an amazing cleansing took place. The filthy words had been washed away by the "soap" of God's Word.

2. The Bible can actually keep us from sinning (Ps. 119:9, 11). The Word of God is placed into our conscious and unconscious minds as we read it. Whenever a temptation to sin occurs, the Holy Spirit is able to draw upon a certain verse or passage to keep us from giving in to the sin. He can use the passage to remind us of what God expects, or He may use it to actually remove our desire to sin.

3. The Bible brings joy to the Christian (Ps. 119:14). Psychologists have helped us realize that many of our actions are affected by our attitudes. If we are basically joyful, then many of our decisions will be positive ones. If we are depressed or pessimistic, even the smallest hills can seem like mountains. God's Word helps us keep a proper perspective on life so that true joy may be a guiding life-force.

4. The Bible judges the motives of our hearts (Heb. 4:12). Have you ever wondered whether you were serving the Lord out of a pure motive or for selfish reasons? Have you wondered if the pride you feel when you are complimented for some Christian attribute is acceptable to God? The Word of God is a sharp, two-edged sword that the Holy Spirit can use to help us discern what is from the old nature and what is from the new nature.

5. The Bible gives the Christian guidance

(Ps. 119:105). In this world of darkness, when we must often walk down ways that are not always clear, it is helpful to realize the importance that the Lord places on His Word. As we take each new step, He is ready to reveal to us through the Bible the steps, or stops, we are to take.

6. The Bible warns us of impending dangers (Ps. 19:7–11). Can you imagine what it would be like to drive on today's highways without the benefit of the traffic signs which warn of curves in the road, one-lane bridges ahead, holes in the road, or dead-end streets? The Bible is God's means of warning us about potholes and detours to avoid. It clearly shows us which bridges are out and what is a dead-end street.

7. The Bible gives us encouragement and hope (Rom. 15:4). When the storms of life toss us about, it is God's Word that helps us keep our hopes up. When every other bit of information we are receiving is discouraging, it is the Word of God that comes through with the good news that God is still on His throne.

8. The Bible is one means by which the Lord teaches us how He wants us to live (2 Tim. 3:16–17). Everywhere we turn, people are giving us advice as to what to do or what to believe if we want to be happy. The only instruction that is reliable is what is found in the pages of the Bible. All of our theology must be based on the Word of God if we are to be successful in our attempts to grow as Christians.

9. The Bible is a sword against the attacks of Satan (Eph. 6:17; Matt. 4:10–11). If you study carefully the temptation experience of Jesus in the wilderness, you will soon notice that each time Jesus was tempted by Satan He quoted Scripture. He also knew when Satan was quoting the Bible out of context.

• • • • •

Clearly, reading the Bible ought to be a beneficial exercise. Are you finding it so?

HOW ARE YOU BENEFITING FROM YOUR BIBLE STUDY?

Rate yourself as to how well you think you are doing—on a scale of 1 to 5:

Key: 1 = Much Benefit, 2 = Average Benefit,
     3 = Some Benefit, 4 = Little Benefit,
     5 = No Benefit.

	1	2	3	4	5
1. Cleansing from sin and contamination					
2. Being kept from sinning					
3. Joy and a positive attitude					
4. Analyzing my motives					
5. Guidance					
6. Warning of danger					
7. Encouragement and hope					
8. Understanding the will of God for my life					
9. Overcoming Satan					

After completing the chart, decide on areas where you need improvement. Try to determine if your weaknesses are in procedure, time, place, organization, or another area. Read the following suggestions for Bible study to gain insight, then try to make the necessary changes in your own Bible study. God wants you to benefit fully from the study of His Word.

GENERAL SUGGESTIONS FOR BIBLE STUDY

Bible study is like most of the other important things in our lives: there has to be some kind of regular plan after we make the initial commitment to the endeavor. If we decide we need to go on a diet, we make the initial commitment and then we make specific plans for implementation. Commitment without planning will not benefit us much.

1. Set a specific time and place for your Bible study. I have found the early morning, before I have to face the challenges of the day, to be the best time. Try it, and see if that is not the same for you. But any set time is better than no time, and it is likely that if it is not a regularly scheduled appointment with God it will often be forgotten. Also remember that ten minutes a day is better than one hour once a week.

2. Spend time alone in Bible study. Although it is very important for a Christian to have times when he studies the Bible with others or has family devotions, nothing can take the place of time alone with God. Some-

times the Lord has a special word He wants to say just to you.

3. Always pray for the guidance of the Holy Spirit in understanding the Scripture. He has been given to us as the Great Teacher and Interpreter of the Word of God. Ask Him to calm your heart and mind so that you may be able to hear His still, small voice.

4. Learn how to meditate on the Word of God and apply it to your own life and situation. Don't read a large quantity of material at such a fast pace that you do not have time to think about how it relates to your own life. And don't settle for knowledge of facts only. Ask the Lord to show you how this particular verse or passage can help you live a better Christian life today.

5. Vary your methods of Bible study. Try to keep from getting into a rut or meaningless routine. Even strawberry shortcake would get boring if you had it every day.

6. Memorize the Scripture. Memorization is a very helpful way to benefit spiritually from Bible study. An excellent place to start is with Bible promises. With these promises planted firmly in your memory, it will be easier for you to claim them and for the Holy Spirit to bring them to your mind. Don't be deceived into thinking that you cannot memorize the Bible. Constant reading of the promises will help you learn them. After all, it is unlikely that you ever made an attempt to memorize TV commercials, but you have probably learned many of the familiar phrases simply from con-

stant exposure.

7. Read the Bible whenever you have some spare time. Even though you have a regular time for personal Bible study, it is always helpful to read the Bible again later if you have the time. Carry a pocket-size New Testament with you for reading in the doctor's office, etc. Keep a Bible by your lounge chair, and read a chapter or two after you finish the newspaper. Memorize verses while driving to work or waiting in traffic on the freeway. Put a cassette tape of a Bible passage in your car's tape player and listen to it as you travel.

SPECIFIC METHODS FOR ENHANCING YOUR BIBLE STUDY

There are many different ways to study the Scripture that can make it more meaningful to you. Try several until you discover the ones that you like the most. Be sure to vary your methods, however, to keep your study from becoming monotonous. Many people read their Bibles regularly because they feel they should but readily admit that they are not receiving the blessing they desire.

1. Read a chapter a day of a certain book. The Gospels are a good place to start since they deal with the life and teachings of our Lord. Psalms and Proverbs are other helpful sources of instruction for day-to-day living. Vary your reading to include some of the books in the New Testament and then some of those in the Old Testament.

2. Utilize different translations. Study a book or chapter from one translation, and then read it from another translation. Using one of the parallel Bibles that has the translations side by side is also helpful.

3. Make one of your Bible study days "memorization" day. Spend the Bible study portion of your quiet time memorizing a verse and thinking about its particular meaning in your life. Make plans to share that verse and its personal meaning for you with someone else that day.

4. Study special topics. Using a Bible concordance, look up topics of special interest to you, such as prayer, faith, the will of God, courage, Bible promises, etc. Spend several days on the topic you are studying.

5. Begin your own Bible-verse coloring system. Using soft-lead colored pencils, begin coloring certain verses or passages on topics or people as you study them. This is a great way to preserve your Bible study for future use. Marking Bible promises is a good way to start.

6. Study various Bible characters in order to learn from their successes or mistakes. Use your concordance to look up a name, and then spend time reading the references about this Bible personality. Again, don't forget to apply to your life what you learn.

7. Use helpful Bible study books or devotional books. There are many devotional books and Bible study books on the market. Ask some other Christians for their advice in this area, or spend some time browsing through

the devotional section of a Christian bookstore. One word of caution: Be sure that you do not have so many devotional books that you spend more time reading *them* than you do the Bible itself.

8. Have a note-taking system of some kind. It is a widely known fact that we all have a tendency to forget more than we remember. Be sure to take the time to make some notes, keep a journal, etc., to help you retain what you are learning.

Remember that Bible study can be fun and exciting, not dull and boring. Whenever you hear about different methods others are using, try them out. Variety is the spice of life. Even an excellent method can be overworked. And be sure to have a regular checkup to see how you are progressing in this area of your spiritual growth.

CHAPTER TWO

CHECKING UP ON YOUR PRAYER LIFE

Prayer is a conversation between a Christian and his Lord, a time of sharing and love that benefits both communicators. Since we are taught prayers to say when we are children, it is not unusual to hear adults praying what are often merely statements rather than heartfelt conversation. We learn to say a blessing at the table and our "Now I lay me down to sleep" when we retire at night, and it is difficult to overcome this habit of merely saying things to God.

As we listen to prayers prayed out loud in church we hear certain key phrases repeated, such as "Lead, guide, and direct us," "Lord, bless the missionaries," "Forgive us our many sins," and "Bless those who couldn't be with us today." None of these requests are unfounded or unworthy to bring to God. The problem occurs if they have become merely phrases that we are saying as our prayers.

One of the best ways for us to make some progress in our prayer life is to try to come to a better understanding of the elements that should be included in a well-balanced prayer life. Again, the Scripture must be our guide.

TYPES OF PRAYER

An infant is limited in his ability to communicate his wishes to his parents. We learn how to interpret his fussiness and crying, and we try our best to meet his needs. As he continues to grow, however, we expect his communication abilities to increase. We want him to be able to express both his needs and his feelings to us.

As we grow in the Christian life, the Lord likewise expects us to grow in our ability to communicate. Among the first lessons we must learn is what types of communication in prayer are expected.

1. Petition (1 Jn. 5:14–15). Often the first prayer we learn to pray is one in which we ask for something we want, a "specific request." The Lord wants us to voice our desires to Him, even though He knows what we want and need before we ask. He wants to bless us and show His love to us by giving us the things we request that are within His will.

2. Intercession (1 Tim. 2:1). The Lord wants us to grow beyond the boundary of only praying for ourselves and to expand our requests into prayer for others. God wants us to be channels through whom He can pour out His power and blessings on others.

3. Confession (1 Jn. 1:9). Jesus paid the full price for all of our sins when He died on

the cross. But we still become stained with sin from both our old Adamic nature and the world around us. Confession, "admitting to God the mistakes and sins we have committed, asking for and claiming His forgiveness," is a vital part of the prayer life of a growing Christian.

4. Supplication (Eph. 6:18; Phil. 4:6). There are times in our lives when we urgently need God's aid but do not know specifically what it is that we need. Or we are unsure what other people's needs are. This is the time that supplication, the "Oh, help!" prayer, is the most beneficial. One encouraging word is the promise that the Holy Spirit will take these supplications to the Throne of Grace and interpret them for us (Rom. 8:20).

5. Thanksgiving (Eph. 5:20). God also looks for a grateful heart in the lives of His children. He knows we need to declare our appreciation for His goodness to us. A heart filled with gratitude is a joyful heart. The songwriter expressed it well in the hymn chorus, "Count your many blessings; name them. . . ."

6. Praise (Ps. 103:1). In addition to being grateful for what the Lord has done for us, it is important for us to express our love and devotion to Him for who He is. Surely a parent's heart would be broken if he received a sign of love from his children only when he gave them a present or did something nice for them. What a thrill to a father's heart when a son or daughter, for no particular reason, gives him a big hug and kiss along with a

simple "I love you, Dad." Surely the heart of our loving Heavenly Father is just as thrilled when we express our love to Him.

7. Commitment (Mk. 14:36b). Our Lord wants so much for us to "give control of our life and our concerns" to Him. Because He has given us a free will that can choose to say "no" to Him, it is always safest for us to offer a prayer of commitment to Him every day, surrendering all choices of the day into His wise control. He will not force us to do His will; He lovingly waits for us to realize that the happiest place for us to be is in the center of His will.

8. Communion. When we love someone, we enjoy being with him or her. We may be talking or listening or just enjoying one another's company. Our relationship with the Lord should also include these characteristics. We should enjoy being in His presence, whether or not we are talking to Him or listening to Him speak to us.

It is important for us to have all of the above types of prayer in our prayer life if we are to be maturing Christians.

DO YOU HAVE A WELL-BALANCED
PRAYER LIFE?

Rate yourself as to how much you are including the various kinds of prayer in your own prayer life:

Kind of Prayer	Use Often	Use Some	Rarely Use	Never Use
1. Petition				
2. Intercession				
3. Confession				
4. Supplication				
5. Thanksgiving				
6. Praise				
7. Commitment				
8. Communion				

After completing the chart, decide on areas where you need improvement and begin working on these, both in your private prayer life and when you pray in public. Don't be satisfied until you feel comfortable using all kinds of prayer and until you have reached a good balance.

THINGS WE CAN PRAY FOR OR ABOUT

In addition to being certain we have a balance in the kinds of prayer we are utilizing, we must also be certain that the matters we present to God are acceptable. Of course, it is understood that we can discuss with our Father anything that concerns us, but the Bible gives us some specific guidelines that help us focus.

We can pray for help and strength if we are afflicted, ill-treated, or suffering evil (Jas. 5:13). God also tells us it is permissible to pray for those who are sick (Jas. 5:14–15). We need to pray for others when they fall into sin, that they may be healed and restored to a spiritual tone of mind and heart (Jas. 5:19–20).

We are allowed to pray about the weather if it is something that will bring glory to the Lord (Jas. 5:17–18). We are instructed to pray for the lost (Rom. 10:1; 1 Tim. 2:1–4) and for men in authority (1 Tim. 2:1–2).

Our prayer life should include asking that other Christians might have opportunity and boldness to witness (Eph. 6:19; Col. 4:3). We also need to intercede for our fellow Christians, that they may have spiritual wisdom and understanding. This includes knowing the Lord and His will, walking in His love, being fruitful, and knowing His wonderful provisions for His children (Eph. 1:16–20; Col. 1:9–11; Col. 4:12; 1 Thess. 5:23; Jas. 1:5). In addition, He wants us to pray for laborers for His harvest (Matt. 9:38).

If we are to have a well-balanced prayer life, we must learn to pray for our enemies (Matt. 5:44; Acts 7:60). We are expected to pray that the Holy Spirit fill us (Acts 4:29–31; Eph. 3:14–19) and to be praying for the return of the Lord (Rev. 22:20). The Lord expects us to include confession in our prayers (1 Jn. 1:9) as well as a prayer to keep us from the temptation to sin (Matt. 26:41).

The Bible reveals to us our responsibilities in praying for protection in warfare (Ps. 20), for people to be delivered from bondage (Acts 12:5), and for protection from evildoers (Ps. 59:1–2; Ps. 64:2).

The above list is by no means exhaustive, but it is certainly a good place to begin as we try to improve our prayer life. How would you rate yourself in the above areas? Where do you need to improve? What are you overlooking as you talk with God?

WHEN PRAYERS GO UNANSWERED

None of us likes to think that there is a possibility that our prayers may go unanswered. We take comfort in the belief that God will always answer our prayers, no matter what. A closer examination of the biblical teachings on the subject will help us come to a better understanding in this area. We may have been taught that God always answers prayers: yes, no, or wait. But are there times when He does not answer at all?

1. Sin and disobedience affect prayer. God did not answer Joshua's prayer for military help for the nation of Israel because of the sin of Achan, one of their people (Josh. 7). Moses was not allowed to enter the promised land because of his disobedience (Num. 20:12). David's request to God to spare the child that was born because of his sinful union with Bathsheba was not honored (2 Sam. 12). The psalmist tells us that God will not hear us if we regard iniquity in our hearts (Ps. 66:18). Sin disrupts fellowship between us and a holy God. We must be cleansed vessels when we approach the throne of God in prayer (1 Jn. 1:8–10).

2. Sometimes God wants to strengthen our faith. Paul begged the Lord to remove the thorn in the flesh that he suffered. The Lord told him that He would not answer that request because it would be more beneficial for Paul's spiritual life to keep the thorn (2 Cor. 12:7–9). Many times the Lord will say no, or fail to answer our prayers the way we ask Him to, in

order that we may grow in our spiritual lives.

3. Prayers go unanswered when we pray wrongly. If we are praying to impress others and not from the heart, God will not answer us (Matt. 6:5). If we are just praying words that have no meaning to us, our prayers will not be answered (Matt. 6:7). If we are praying selfishly, and not for things that will bring glory to God, our praying is useless (Jas. 4:2–3).

4. Unbelief hinders our prayers. Jesus Himself was unable to perform some miracles among the people to whom He ministered because of their lack of faith (Mk. 6:5–6). James reminds us that we cannot expect to receive answers to our prayers if we are wavering and doubting (Jas. 1:6–7). We must realize, however, that we can pray for the Lord to strengthen our faith. Belief is a result of claiming the promises of God, not some sort of mental gymnastics where we talk ourselves into believing something. Many Christians have erred at this point, and their faith in Christ has been hurt.

5. Our relationship with others can hinder our prayer life. Jesus tells us in the Sermon on the Mount that our relationship with another person is so important that we must get that right before we even come to the altar to present our gifts (Matt. 5:23–24). Many times our prayers are not heard or answered because we are out of fellowship with another Christian. It is easy to hold a grudge, but as long as it is being held we can expect our prayer life to be adversely affected.

Unfortunately, many of us are not progressing in our spiritual lives because of a weak
prayer life. We may be yielding repeatedly to
the same temptations. We may be plagued by
fears and anxieties. We may be suffering con-
fusion concerning God's will in some area of
our lives. A good way to see some progress in
these and other areas is to make certain we
are including the above areas of prayer in our
daily prayer time.

Have some of your prayers gone unanswered? Are you still struggling in areas in
which you should be experiencing victory?
Can you determine what the cause or problem
may be? Could it be a weak prayer life or
weakness in one of the prayer areas?

WHY PRAY IN JESUS' NAME?

I was not a Christian very long before I
noticed that people who voiced public prayers
were ending their prayers with such phrases
as "In Jesus' name," "For Jesus' sake," etc. I
am certain I may have wondered at the time
why they were ending with this phrase prior
to saying "Amen," but I did not ask anyone. I
proceeded to learn "the correct way to do
things" as a Christian even though I did not
know the reason why it was being done. As
the years passed, however, and I became more
inquisitive, I decided to find out why we Christians end our prayers the way we do.

I discovered that there are basically three
reasons why we use the phrase "In Jesus'

name," or some variation of it.

1. We are commanded to pray that way. Jesus Himself instructs us to ask the Father in His name (Jn. 14:13–14; 15:16; 16:23–24). It is because of Christ's sacrifice on Calvary that we can even approach the Throne of Grace. He is our mediator with God the Father. Our prayers must be in His power and by His authority if they are to be effective. They must also be according to His will and His nature and for His glory before they will be answered.

2. Such a prayer-ending is for our benefit— that we be reminded of His supremacy in all we ask. When we end a prayer in the name of Jesus it is a reminder to us that we are asking only for that which is in accordance with the divine will of the Father. In essence we are saying, "Lord, anything I have just requested, please ignore or overlook if it is not in Your will and for Your glory." We need the reminder of such a prayer; we would have no right of our own even to be talking with the God of the universe if it were not for Jesus.

This type of closing, if prayed from the heart and not simply something we mention by rote at the end of a prayer, can lead us not to pray selfishly. It will also cancel out a lot of unnecessary prayer!

3. Such a prayer is a testimony to others. By refusing to end a prayer with only an "Amen," we are declaring to whom we belong and on whom we depend. We give testimony to all listening that Jesus is the only mediator

between God and man. We distinguish ourselves from non-Christians. We must realize, however, that not all who use the phrase are necessarily using it sincerely.

When we pray "In Jesus' name," it is not a phrase we wave like a magic wand in order that God may give us whatever we ask. We must be in a vital relationship with Christ and praying from the heart and with the will before this phrase will mean what it is intended to mean.

HOW DOES GOD SPEAK TO US?

I recently had the occasion to be counseling a college student who is deaf. She had lost her hearing as a result of measles when she was in the first grade. She could speak to me since she had learned to talk before she lost her hearing. The difficulty I had in this counseling session, however, was speaking back to her. I finally overcame the difficulty by typing my remarks onto a computer screen.

I cannot help but wonder if some of our prayer lives are like that. We can talk perfectly well to God and can relate what is on our hearts to Him, but we are deaf or hard of hearing when it comes to listening to Him. I have yet to see a message from Him on my computer screen, but there are some definite ways He is trying to communicate with us—if only we would learn to listen.

1. He speaks through His Word. God's message for us is clearly written in the Bible. And

He has given us the Holy Spirit as our teacher to help us understand the message. Many of us are not availing ourselves of this opportunity to hear what God is trying to say to us. If I had typed a message for the deaf student to read and she refused to look at the computer monitor, my message would never have reached her.

2. He speaks through a still, small voice to our hearts. The way that God speaks to us in our innermost beings is a most difficult one to explain. It is about as difficult as trying to explain how we know that we are in love. Much of the discerning of this internal peace— this assurance concerning His will—comes as we continue to walk with the Lord and under- stand how He deals with us. We learn to know His heart like we learn to know the heart and wishes of a close loved one.

3. God speaks through external circum- stances. The Lord will often speak to us through other people, through our abilities and interests, through open and closed doors, and through sermons and books or other Christian materials. Some of us feel that if we really enjoy doing something, or are good at something, it cannot possibly be God's will for us to do it. Because of our mistaken idea of what Jesus meant when He said, "Take up your cross and follow Me," we feel that the will of God most certainly involves doing some- thing we hate to do. Not so. Many times the Lord is attempting to lead us to use the talent or ability He has given us in such a way as to

glorify Him.

The heart that seeks after a closer walk with the Lord can be assured that the Lord will do His part to make His messages clear. We need to learn to listen attentively for what He is trying to say to us. All of the above methods must be used in conjunction with each other in order for us to be assured that it is God who is speaking to us. In other words, God will not speak a word to us in our hearts that is contrary to His written Word. Nor should we pay attention to any human counsel if it conflicts with our promptings from His Spirit.

Prayer is a two-way communication. It is probably more important to work on the listening aspect of prayer than on the talking aspect. But both are important if we are to continue making progress in our spiritual growth. How are you doing in the listening aspect of prayer?

CLAIM WHAT GOD HAS ALREADY PROMISED

I recently led a Bible study on prayer in the church where I serve as bi-vocational Minister of Education. In the midst of the study I began to see an area of prayer that I had never really studied before. We were examining the effectiveness of our corporate and private prayer lives and, specifically, some of the "familiar phrases" we hear and use so often. We had our eyes opened as to the incorrectness of some of the ways we were phrasing our prayers. Before I share with you some of the things we discovered, take the following test.

CORRECT/INCORRECT PRAYER PHRASES

Mark the following prayer phrases as to their correctness or incorrectness according to the Bible. After marking your answers, check your answers by the appropriate Bible verse.

	Incorrect	Correct
1. "Lord, be with me today." Heb. 13:5b; Isa. 43:2,5	☐	☐
2. "Lead, guide, and direct us." Ps. 32:8	☐	☐
3. "Forgive us when we fail You." 1 Jn. 1:9	☐	☐
4. "Be with the missionaries today." Matt. 28:19–20	☐	☐
5. "If I should die before I wake, I pray the Lord my soul to take." Jn. 11:25	☐	☐
6. "Send Your Holy Spirit into our midst." Jn. 7:38–39; 3:3–6	☐	☐

	Incorrect	Correct

7. "May Your Spirit come down upon us today."
   Jn. 14:16–17

8. "Fill us with Your Holy Spirit."
   Eph. 5:18; 4:30; Jn. 7:38–39

9. "Bless my enemies, Lord."
   Matt. 5:44–48; Rom. 12:14–21

10. "Give us strength for the task."
    Ps. 27:1; 28:7; 29:11; 46:1; Isa. 41:10; Deut. 33:25

11. "Don't forgive me, Lord, if there is someone I haven't forgiven."
    Mk. 11: 25–26; Matt. 6:14–15

12. "Lord, teach us to pray."
    Lk. 11:1

13. "Hear our prayer, O Lord."
    1 Jn. 5:14–15; Isa. 58:9; 65:24

14. "Please save my husband."
    Jn. 16:7–11; Rev. 22:17; Matt. 18:14; 2 Pet. 3:9

How did you do? If you are like our Bible study group, you discovered that you have been phrasing some of your prayers incorrectly. We came to the conclusion that we need to be claiming God's promises more and thanking Him for what He has already given us. We found that we had been spending a lot of time asking the Lord for what He said we already possessed! Many of our petitions turned into praise and thanksgiving and appropriating what was promised to us.

Another word of warning: Do not get discouraged if you have been praying the wrong way. God is not as concerned about *how* we pray as He is *that* we pray. But, of course, if we want to grow in our prayer life we certainly want to learn how to do it as correctly as possible. The changeover may seem awkward at first, but the benefits will be worth it in the long run. If I have a checking account at the bank, I need to know the most efficient way to benefit from this service. I may be able to obtain the money in several different ways, but when I need it I want it to be as accessible as possible! Yes, God's blessings and strength are available to us at all times, but I certainly want to know the best way to be both a recipient and a channel through whom others may be blessed.

Notes

CHAPTER THREE

OBEDIENCE TO THE LORDSHIP OF CHRIST

The Bible declares our Savior to be the Lord Jesus Christ. So when we invited Jesus into our lives to be our Savior, He also entered to be our Lord. It is not possible to have Jesus only as our Savior; He is also Lord. An important practical question arises, however, regarding our obedience to His Lordship. Before we can begin to grasp the significance of His Lordship and evaluate just how obedient we are to Him, it is necessary to understand some facts about our own nature.

UNDERSTANDING OUR NATURE

In 1 Thessalonians 5:23, Paul is making a request to the Lord for his Christian friends in Thessalonica. He is asking the Lord to preserve their bodies, souls and spirits until His return. It is certainly clear that we are complex individuals with many interacting parts, but a simplification of the concept of this verse may give us some help as we progress toward Jesus being the Lord of our lives. The following diagram may help.

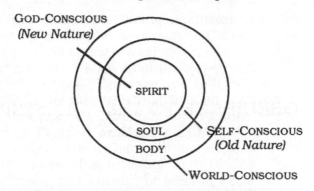

GOD-CONSCIOUS
(New Nature)

SPIRIT

SOUL

BODY

SELF-CONSCIOUS
(Old Nature)

WORLD-CONSCIOUS

A LOOK AT THREE KINDS OF PEOPLE

The *natural man,* more commonly termed a lost sinner, does not understand spiritual things or accept spiritual truths. He is dead in sin, doomed, lost. Even though he is unaware of it, he is walking according to the world system; he is following and obeying Satan and is under his influence and control. He is under God's wrath and is condemned already because of his refusal to accept Christ into his life (1 Cor. 2:14; Eph. 2:1–3; Jn. 3:3,17–18).

The *carnal man,* or baby Christian, is immature spiritually. This may be due to the fact that he is a new Christian, or it may be that he just has not known or desired to grow into spiritual maturity. The old, carnal nature predominates. Decisions are made without consulting the Lord. Traits such as lying, anger, stealing, evil speaking, bitterness, resentment and hatred predominate. The carnal Christian is unable to understand many spiritual truths, for he is still feeding on spiritual *milk,* the *basics* of the Christian life. Selfishness, jealousy, wanting one's own way, and being unkind and unloving are the attitudes and the behavior that are frequently noticed in his life (1 Cor. 3:1–3; Eph. 4:24–32).

The *spiritual man,* as described in the Bible, has spiritual insight that baffles the unbeliever. He has the assurance that he is a child of God, and he humbly seeks to restore those who fall into sin. The most conspicuous evidence of his new condition is the spiritual fruit that is manifested in his life: love, joy, peace, longsuffering, gentleness, goodness, faith, meekness and self-control (1 Cor. 2:15–16; Gal. 5:22–23; 6:1; Rom. 8:16). (See Chapter Six for more information on spiritual fruit.)

Another way to help us understand the differences in the above persons is as follows:

✝ = CHRIST   S = SELF

S   =   NATURAL MAN
Christ is outside the life;
Self is in the driver's seat

S ✝ =   CARNAL MAN
Christ is in the life, but
Self is in the driver's seat

✝ S =   SPIRITUAL MAN
Christ is both in the life
and in the driver's seat

As lost individuals we are "riding down the highway of life" in a car driven by us wherever we want to take it. If we are fortunate enough to realize that we are traveling on a road that leads only to destruction, we invite Christ into the car to make the journey with us, and we begin our travel on a different road. We are now carnal, or new, Christians. Christ is in the life, but we are still driving the car. We may ask for His advice and suggestions, but basically we are still in control.

If we continue to mature in our Christian life, it will undoubtedly dawn upon us that it would be better for us to become the passenger and invite Jesus to be the driver. Whenever we get to that point, we are allowing Him to be the Lord of our lives. Of course, it would be wonderful if there were no longer any problems after that decision. Unfortunately, that is not the case. There is a lifelong struggle to allow Him the privilege of remaining at the wheel while we attempt not to be a back-seat driver.

It will be helpful for us to study the following diagram as we learn how to allow Jesus to be Lord of our lives and therefore begin to function as spiritual Christians.

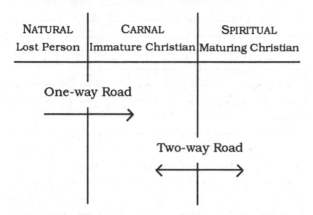

Moving from natural to carnal (lost to saved) is a one-way street (——>). Once a person has become a Christian, he does not have to worry about slipping back into the natural state (Jn. 10:27–28). The roadway between carnal and spiritual, however, is a two-way street (<——>). If a person continues to grow as a Christian, allows Jesus to be Lord of his life—and hence manifests spiritual fruit—he moves from the carnal state to the spiritual state. Because our old nature never changes or improves, however, whenever we take back the control of our life, we risk slipping back into a carnal condition.

MOVING FROM NATURAL TO CARNAL

It is necessary for each person to pass from natural man to carnal man before progressing on to spiritual man. Unfortunately, many people never leave the natural state.

In order for anyone to move from natural (lost) to carnal (saved), there are four basic steps:

1. The person must first recognize his need. He must realize that his sin has separated him from God and nothing he can do on his own will remove the penalty of death. He must come to understand that all sin separates from God (Isa. 59:2; Rom. 3:23), not just the breaking of the "big 10" (the Ten Commandments, Exodus 20).

2. He must repent of his sin, turn from it, and ask God to forgive him and cleanse him. He must have the attitude of wanting to remove the sin entirely from his life (Lk. 24:47; Acts 17:30; 2 Pet. 3:9; 1 Jn. 1:9).

3. He must realize God's provision for his salvation from sin. God sent Jesus to pay the price for all sin. While He hung on the cross, Christ Himself suffered separation from a holy God. The payment has been made for all who are willing to accept it (Jn. 3:16; Rom. 6:23).

4. He must by an act of faith receive Christ into his life (Acts 20:21; Rev. 3:20; Jn. 1:12).

When a person has been through the above steps, God transfers him from the natural state to the baby Christian, or carnal, state. Whether he stays in the carnal state or moves on to the spiritual state is dependent upon his cooperation with the Spirit of God who now lives within him (Jn. 16:13; Rom. 8:9).

MOVING FROM CARNAL TO SPIRITUAL

As a Christian begins to grow spiritually, it soon becomes evident that the tendency to sin has not been removed. The continual struggle to go back to the world's standards is ever present with us. It is obvious that our "old man" is very much alive and desires to control our life and actions. Paul speaks of this struggle between the old and new natures in the seventh chapter of Romans. The things we want to do, we do not do. And the behavior we wish we were not exhibiting is the very behavior we see in our life.

How can we learn to consistently respond to the Lord obediently, rather than disobeying? How can we allow the spiritual part of our nature to be predominant?

1. We have to recognize our need. If we are satisfied with our present level of spirituality we will see no need to go any further. It is easy to compare our progress in the Christian life with that of others and thereby feel better about where we are. It is easy to rationalize our actions and attitudes or give in to discouragement and defeat. The first thing we need to do before we will get anywhere is to realize that we must keep pressing on and growing in Christ.

2. We need to repent of our carnality. When

we recognize that our carnal man has been in control of our lives, we need to repent of this sin and ask the Lord to forgive us and cleanse us. I used to think that I had to control the old nature or to re-educate it to act in a Christian manner. After years of trying this approach and failing, I began to see the futility of that tactic. It is as impossible for us to control our old nature as it is for a lost person to save himself.

3. We must yield to the Holy Spirit. The Holy Spirit comes to dwell within us as the energizer of our lives. It is He who is to live the Christian life in and through us. It is He alone who can empower us with Himself so that the carnal man is controlled. Some examples at this point may be helpful.

I do not particularly enjoy riding in airplanes, even though I enjoy the benefit of getting somewhere in a hurry. The reason probably stems from the fact that I was in a severe electrical storm during one of my first trips. I find myself trying to help the pilot keep the plane in the air. I mentally help him at take-off and during landing to steady the plane! Of course, you and I both know that I am not affecting the performance of the plane at all, but it certainly makes me feel a lot better to think I am helping some!

I also have this tendency as a Christian. I think I can help the Lord keep my life afloat if I just struggle and try a great deal. I may count to twenty before I speak, or bite my tongue, or practice my sweet smiles—when it is actually the Lord who is producing any spiritual fruit that may be manifested in my life. Surely He must feel like the pilot of the airplane would if I were to brag to all of the passengers that I helped him accomplish a smooth flight! The Lord just smiles, I am sure, and waits for the day when I will come to understand who is really responsible for any success in my life.

Another example that might help us understand the principle we are dealing with is as follows. Pretend that I am holding a sheet of paper up in front of myself. Behind it I have a flashlight that has a control by which I can make the light brighter or dimmer. You cannot see the flashlight, only the paper. When I turn on the light dimly, you will notice a small circle of light on the paper, but mostly you will be aware of the paper. As I increase the brightness of the light, however, you will become more aware of the light and less aware of the paper. The Holy Spirit lives within our bodies of clay. He desires to shine forth His light in such a way that our own natures become less and less obvious to others. It is He who wants to live the Christian life, but He desires to do it through clean and yielded vessels.

4. Once I have recognized my need, repented of my carnality, and recognized the provision of the Holy Spirit in my life, the next step must take place. I must, by the same act of faith I used when I accepted Christ as Savior, make Him Lord of every situation that the carnal man is controlling or wants to control.

An example at this point may be helpful.

In a given situation, I notice that I am re-acting to someone with anger and impatience rather than with love and concern. Immedi-ately I realize the need I have for the spiritual man to be in control. I repent of the attitudes and feelings that have already been evident in my old nature. I ask the Lord to forgive me and cleanse me of the sin of anger and impa-tience. I realize that the Holy Spirit who lives in me has the fruit of love and patience ready for my use. By an act of faith, I ask the Lord to take my anger and impatience and replace it with love and concern. If I am sincere, and if I am willing to release the ugly feelings, the Lord will make the swap immediately.

So often we think we are willing to surren-der our sinful attitudes and feelings when in reality we are rationalizing just why the feel-ings we are having are really justified. Whenever we are willing to yield to His control, He will manifest His Spirit and the fruit of His grace in our lives.

STAYING IN THE SPIRITUAL STATE

There are a number of ways we can be helped to become more willing to progress through the above steps. Our old man is sure to give us a struggle, as he does not like giving up the rights to the throne of our life. What can we do, then, to make this matter of yield-ing to the Holy Spirit a little easier? Some basic principles will be of help at this point.

1. Practice enthroning Christ as Lord of each day and each situation. The first thing you should do each morning upon waking is to give the Lord permission to do whatever He wants to with you that day. Surrender the day to His Lordship. And as different situations arise that cause your old man to attempt to take back the control, recommit those matters to the Lord for His control.

2. Spend time each day in Bible study and prayer. It is absolutely essential that your spiritual nature be fed if it is to be stronger than the old nature. God's Word is powerful, and the Holy Spirit can use it to keep our spiritual plane in the air.

3. Keep your sins confessed up-to-date. One of the ways that the Spirit is short-circuited in our lives is when we sin and fail to confess. The "paper" becomes dirty, so the light of the Lord cannot shine through. He has not left us; He is just not able to work as He desires. And don't forget that a large part of the cleansing process depends upon our willingness to ask others to forgive us when we sin against them. The Lord cannot cleanse us unless our relationships with others are what they should be.

4. Be actively involved in a local church, in fellowship and service. Since we are all part of the body of Christ, it is impossible for us to function as we should if we are "lone-ranger" Christians. The Lord expects us to use our spiritual gifts to help each other grow. My growth as a Christian can have an effect on your obedience to the Lord, and vice versa.

Each of us can be more successful in this goal of spiritual growth when we fellowship with others who are growing too.

5. Step out in faith and begin this walk with the Lord. So many times a lost person will put off accepting Christ as Savior because it looks like it is difficult to do. Until he determines to "give it a try," his having thought about it for ten years will do him no good. The same thing is true for Christians who are considering the walk with Jesus as Lord. Many are afraid to go ahead and give it a try. Some have read books on the subject and heard sermons and seminars espousing the joys of such a relationship, but until they are willing to step out in faith they will not make any progress.

LEARNING HOW TO WALK IN THE SPIRIT

Making Jesus Lord and living under His Lordship is much the same process as learning how to walk.

1. We have to do the walking. No one can do it for us. No matter how well our parents or friends or pastor can walk, we will only benefit when we do our own walking.

2. Walking is done one step at a time. This is often discouraging to us when we want to proceed further down the road to spirituality. We want to take giant steps, go faster than the speed limit, and skip over a lot of the rough places. But this can cause us to stumble.

3. We need strength to walk. I will never

forget an experience I had when in the first grade. I contracted hepatitis, and after six weeks in bed I was so weak I could not walk without assistance. Some of us have "spiritual hepatitis" and have not walked for so long that we will probably need a lot of help at first. One thing we must be certain to do is get the proper diet: God's Word.

4. Walking is a learned behavior. Even though walking has become second nature to most of us, there was a time in our lives when we had to learn how to do it. Our ability to walk spiritually is also a learned behavior. Some of us do not want to do the walking unless it comes without effort. Most of our spiritual walking lessons will involve difficulty.

5. If we do not have any place to go, we will not want to do any walking. Many elderly people who are shut-ins begin to get wobbly in their walking because they do not have anywhere to go and consequently do little walking. If we as Christians do not see the need to progress in our spiritual lives, then it is doubtful that we will be doing much spiritual walking.

6. If we fall or encounter an obstacle when we are walking, we make the necessary adjustments to continue. I have a nephew who is fourteen months old. When he was about ten months of age, his parents tried to coax him to do some walking. After a few falls, he apparently decided that he liked crawling better. He has not tried to walk since! I am certain that the time will come when he will recover

his bravery and join the world of walkers, but for now it is just too much trouble. Some of us Christians act the same way. At one time in our lives we made a noble attempt at walking spiritually. But we either encountered an obstacle or took a fall of some sort, and we have refused to try it again. It may be all right to read about walking, but to actually try it is not a priority.

SCRIPTURAL AID

Some scriptural instructions may be of help to us as we try to be more successful in walking with Jesus as Lord.

1. Walking is an act of faith, just as accepting Christ as Savior was (Col. 2:6). There is a point at which we must come to the end of our own resources and trust Christ's strength. Before we accepted Christ as Savior, our old nature attempted to be acceptable to God on its own merits. We made every effort to be good enough for God to save us. The same temptation exists after we become Christians. Our old nature still tries to convince us that it can produce spiritual qualities of its own that are acceptable to God.

2. It is a righteous walk (Eph. 4:1–3; Rom. 13:13–14). Christ expects us to stay out of the mud puddles of life and to stay on the path He has chosen for us.

It is often amusing to watch a young child as he walks along the sidewalk on a rainy day, going out of his way to walk through all the puddles of water. Thirty years later, however, when he is with business associates, it would be very inappropriate for his behavior to be the same. The Lord expects us to mature in our walk of righteousness.

3. Good works are expected as we make this walk (Eph. 2:10). Our ability to walk is not for our benefit alone. We are to be ministering and serving as we learn how to walk. Walking with the Lord means to be about His business. It is not a self-absorbed journey.

4. It is a walk in the light and not in darkness (Eph. 5:8). Before my neighborhood was equipped with streetlights, I would sometimes begin an evening walk while it was still daylight. One evening, however, I began later, and it was dark before I could make it back to the house. I was walking in total darkness, which was dangerous to me and could also have caused harm to someone else. I was walking, but the lack of light was a problem. As Christians, we can cause harm to ourselves and others if we walk about in darkness. If we have no sense of direction or are away from the light of the Father's love, problems can arise.

5. It is a walk of love (Eph. 5:2). I watched a session of the Oprah Winfrey show one afternoon when the guests were discussing witchcraft. As is customary on the program, guests of opposing viewpoints had been asked to present their opinions on the topic. I was disappointed that the woman "witch" presented her beliefs in a more loving spirit than did the

Christian minister present. 1 Corinthians 13 should be our guideline for this walk of love. Whether we are held up in traffic or standing in a long line at the grocery store, our spirit of love and patience should be evident to all who see us.

6. It is a careful walk (Eph. 5:15–16). You probably have occasionally been walking in a mall or grocery store when someone, not watching where he was going, ran into you. It is easy for us as Christians to be so concerned about our own lives that we run into some unsuspecting person with an unkind word or abrupt attitude.

7. We are to walk as Jesus walked (Col. 1:10; 1 Jn. 2:6). If ever a question arises as to whether we are walking as a Christian ought, we should ask ourselves, "What would Jesus do in this situation?" Jesus always walked in a way that would please His Father. That should be the goal of our lives.

8. We are to walk according to the Lord's commandments (2 Jn. 6). Imagine what it would be like to travel a highway that had no road signs to warn us. We might think it would be nice not to have to maintain a certain speed, but we would quickly change our minds as to the value of road signs if we ran off the road on an unmarked curve or drove into a river when the "bridge out" sign was not present. God has given us road signs in the form of commandments and instructions in His Word. If we ignore them or refuse to obey them, our journey along the road to spiritual

maturity will be hazardous.

9. It is a joyful walk (Eph. 5:18–20). One result of our walking with Jesus as Lord ought to be an overflowing joy, produced by His Spirit who dwells in us. It is surely fitting that we should express our love and thankfulness to Him, and one ideal way of doing this is through psalms, hymns and song of praise—"making melody in your heart to the Lord."

The Lord knew that our journey through this life would be one of total disaster if we were left to live the Christian life in our own strength. For Him to be our coach on the sidelines or even a fellow player in the game would certainly be of some help. But He knew the only way we could accomplish His will for us and experience the peace and satisfaction He wants for us was to come and live inside us. Allowing Him to live in and through us is to experience fullness of life. He is Lord. He would have us realize and respond and benefit from that realization. How are you doing in your obedience to the Lordship of Christ?

LORDSHIP INVENTORY

	YES	NO	UNSURE
1. I have identified my basic spiritual condition as natural, carnal or spiritual.	☐	☐	☐
2. I understand how a person moves from a natural to a carnal state.	☐	☐	☐
3. I understand how a person moves from a carnal to a spiritual state.	☐	☐	☐
4. I have identified some areas in my life which need working on, and I intend to take the necessary steps to be more spiritual.	☐	☐	☐

STAYING IN THE SPIRITUAL CATEGORY

	DOING GREAT	DOING OKAY	BELOW PAR	LITTLE/ NONE
1. I am enthroning Christ as Lord of each day and each situation.				
2. I am spending time each day in Bible study and prayer.				
3. I am keeping my sins confessed up-to-date and repenting of them.				
4. I am actively involved in a local church, in fellowship and service.				
5. I am making an active attempt to be a spiritual Christian.				

Specific plans to help in my growth:

Notes

CHAPTER FOUR

WHO'S WINNING THE SPIRITUAL BATTLE?

One of the startling facts that a Christian who is trying to grow to spiritual maturity soon realizes is that there are battles to win in addition to the one being waged within himself. So much of our time can be spent seeking in the power of the Spirit to keep our old nature under control, however, that we may forget that there are momentous battles being fought on another battlefield.

Satan, the prince of darkness, is waging a persistent battle against us as God's children—for several basic reasons. Upset that we are no longer a part of his kingdom, he certainly does not want us influencing others to desert him. So he aims to silence our testimony and to ruin our living witness. He also wants very much to keep us from enjoying our walk with the Lord while we are here on earth. Therefore he and his demons are constantly attacking Christians, but often in such beguiling ways that many of us are not even aware that there is a battle being fought!

Happily, we do not have to fully understand the devil's strategies in order to prevail. Whatever Satan's tactics, God knows our needs and has already provided us with the essentials for victory.

A LOOK AT THE ARMOR

For us to be successful in the fight against Satan, we need to be aware of the armor that God has provided for us as Christians to wear. The Apostle Paul informs us of this in Ephesians, chapter 6. Since he was a prisoner when he wrote this epistle, he chose to describe the clothing that the Christian is to wear using as his illustration the armor worn by his Roman guards.

1. *Helmet of salvation.* The Roman soldier needed a helmet in order to protect his head. One well-placed blow on the head would either knock him out or kill him. In either case, he would be in no condition to engage in battle! We as Christians need our helmet to protect our head—the source of our thought-life and the seat of our decisions.

Paul states that the Christian's helmet is salvation. Salvation, or being delivered from sin, is a three-fold process. When we accept Christ as Savior, in essence we are saved in three ways:

(a) We *are* delivered from the *penalty* of sin. We need never worry about having to go to hell as the consequence of our sins.

(b) We are assured that we *will be* saved from the *presence* of sin when we finally get to heaven.

(c) We are presently *being* saved from the *power* of sin in this world as we allow the Spirit of God to live out His life through us.

It is in this third realm that we have our biggest struggles today. Our helmet will never fall off; we cannot lose our salvation. But it can slip back on our heads when we allow Satan or self to win any of the battles in our minds or our decisions. Our thought-life must be protected, or many spiritual battles will be lost. What we allow to go into our minds can be the material that makes or breaks us. Impure and sinful input from the media, books, dirty jokes, or others' conversations can pollute our minds and cloud our judgment.

2. *Breastplate of righteousness.* The soldier needed a breastplate to protect his heart and other vital organs. A dart through the heart or a sword in the stomach would end his career! We as Christians need a breastplate to protect our hearts, the seat of the emotions. Many battles we fight with Satan are won or lost by how we feel.

The protection for our emotions is righteousness: right standing with God, and a holy life. If we are out of fellowship with God or have some unconfessed sin in our lives, it is easy for Satan to get at our feelings. He may attack us with feelings of guilt or unworthiness, or his tactic may be to cause us to have feelings of fear or anxiety. The best way to keep him away from our feelings is to carefully guard our righteousness. We need to be certain at all times that there is nothing in our lives that has separated us from God and that all sins have been confessed and cleansed away. Unholiness in any part of our lives exposes our hearts to the attacks of Satan.

3. *Belt of truth.* The belt had a two-fold purpose for the soldier: to keep his breastplate and clothing in place and to hold his sword. If his belt came loose, he was in danger of losing the use of his sword or having his breastplate come loose and get in his way.

Truth is defined in Webster's dictionary as something "honest and faithful." In Greek, it means "steadfastness and certainty." The primary reason we need to have our belts in place today is for the use of the sword. If we are being dishonest in any part of our lives, or if we are unstable in our commitment to the Lord, then our ability to use the Word of God (the sword) against Satan will be hindered. Dishonesty and lack of commitment quench the power of God's Spirit.

4. *Shield of faith.* The soldier needed a large shield in order to keep the darts and arrows shot at him from reaching their target. If he dropped his shield or if it was a small one, he immediately became vulnerable to the attacks of the enemy. Faith for the Christian is "to lean one's personality on God in absolute trust and confidence in His power, wisdom, and goodness." If we fail to exercise this faith, or if our faith is small, then we are vulnerable to the darts that Satan throws at us. The darts of doubt, depression and discouragement are only deflected by the Christian who has strong

faith: a large shield.

5. *Shoes of peace.* The soldier could be wearing all of the pieces of the armor, but without his shoes he would not be able to progress very far due to the rough terrain. Something as minor as a pebble or thorn could completely hinder his ability to fight the enemy. Whenever a person had on his shoes, or sandals, it implied that he was going somewhere, since he would not have them on if he was at home to stay. So the wearing of shoes by a Christian means that he is going somewhere. The Christian's shoes imply that he is on the march against Satan, not just sitting and waiting for the next temptation. Also implied is that the Christian is engaged in trying to rescue others out of the kingdom of Satan— taking the message of God's peace to those who need to hear the gospel.

6. *Sword of the Spirit.* The Roman soldier needed the sword if he was going to be able to make any offensive moves against the enemy. Without a weapon, he would be forced to accept the attacks of the opponent. For the Christian the sword of the Spirit is the Word of God. It is the only offensive weapon we have against Satan. We can learn from the temptations of Jesus: Jesus overcame the onslaughts of the enemy by correctly using Scripture against him (Matt. 4:1–11).

7. *Prayer.* If the soldier was completely dressed in each piece of the armor—including even a nice, sharp sword—but was not breathing, he wouldn't be much good to those in his

regiment! The same is true with us as Christians. If we are not breathing—which is best described in the spiritual realm as ongoing prayer—then we will be absolutely helpless when it comes to our battles with Satan.

KEEPING FULLY DRESSED

One of my nephews, who is two years old, seems to be as happy running around in a diaper as he is when he is dressed up in his Sunday best. If he kicks off his shoes and runs around in his stocking feet, no one seems to be very concerned. This behavior is accepted as natural for someone his age. If, however, when he is thirty years old and working for some company, he decides to go to work only in his underwear, he will quickly discover that what he could do at age two is now unacceptable!

Unfortunately, many Christians feel it is acceptable for them to be wearing the same spiritual diapers they wore when they were first converted. It doesn't seem to bother them that they have not discovered the need for or learned how to put on "adult" clothing. Many have never heard of the armor of God, the adult clothing for the maturing Christian. And many who have become acquainted with the subject have no idea how to "dress themselves" properly.

In the previous section of this chapter we looked at the clothing itself. It is necessary at this point to come to an understanding of how to put on and keep on this armor. It will be helpful if we can answer the following questions.

1. How much of the armor do we need?

A careful reading of Ephesians 6:11 and 13 will reveal that the Apostle Paul stressed that we as Christians need the *whole* armor of God. If we have only a few of the pieces, it will soon become obvious to us that Satan is defeating us in the areas of our lives that are not protected.

2. Why do we need it?

A Christian must be wearing the whole armor of God in order to protect himself against the tricks, strategies and deceits of the devil (vs. 11–12). Satan often disguises himself as an angel of light (2 Cor. 11:14) in order to deceive the Christian into obeying his instructions. Of course, he will tempt us to do any sin he thinks we will yield to, but he also likes to pretend that he is the Holy Spirit in order for us to be led off on a tangent. He does not care if we are religious and are busy doing good things—he just does not want us to be in the center of God's will. He especially does not want us to be aware of his sly tactics. We need all of God's armor if we are to be able to defeat Satan in our lives and to help rescue others who are in his clutches.

3. Where can we get this armor?

Paul makes clear to the Ephesians that this armor they are expected to wear is the armor of *God* (vs. 11, 13). He also stresses that the strength to wear the armor in the conflict against Satan comes as a result of our union with the Lord of power (v. 10). If we receive the armor that God gives us and then try to wear it in our own strength, we will be like the boy David who could not fight the giant Goliath while wearing Saul's armor. The armor is given to us by God, and the strength to wear it and to use it in our spiritual warfare is dependent upon our close union with the Lord.

4. How often do we have to wear it?

It is obvious that a soldier should be dressed for battle whenever there is a time of war. It would be foolish for him to wear the armor one day and then leave it off the next. The same is true for a Christian. The battles with Satan are fought every day. It is urgent, therefore, that the Christian know how to put his armor on every day and how to keep it on. He should be aware when there is a problem about the function of his armor, and he should know how to put a piece back on if he finds he is somehow without it. (More information will be given on this aspect in the later sections of this chapter.)

5. When do we put it on?

When I first accepted the Lord Jesus as my Savior, I was impressed with the necessity of having a daily time of Bible study and prayer. Like many Christians I know, I decided to have this quiet time at night (since I do not consider myself a morning person). I soon realized, however, after a careful study of the passage in Ephesians 6 regarding the armor of God, that I was walking around all day fighting spiritual battles and then coming home to put on my armor to go to bed! At that point in my life I changed my Bible study to the morning, and I have been much more successful in my warfare with Satan.

6. How do we put on the armor?

Putting on the armor is one of the easiest things to do. Keeping it on and using it effectively against Satan are the biggest problems.

When we accepted the Lord as Savior we received the helmet of salvation. Our sins were forgiven, so we were then made righteous in His eyes. The seed of faith was placed in our hearts by the power of the Holy Spirit. The Lord of truth came to live inside of us, and the Living Word became our teacher of the written Word. We were commissioned to share the good news of the gospel (walk with shoes on) and were given the indwelling Holy Spirit who is our strength for life.

It is soon obvious to the maturing Christian, however, that it is very easy to take off the armor God has provided for us. We cannot ever lose our helmet of salvation, but it very often slides over our eyes and we become blinded to the blessings of our relationship with the Lord. Our belt slips down around our knees as we tell a few white lies. Our sword is often left on the nightstand. Our shield of faith has so many holes in it that we are constantly being injured by the poisonous darts of the evil one. Our shoes are left at home as we neglect to witness while making our journey through this life. And our prayer life is so weak that we are barely able to walk as Christians, much less to fight any battles on behalf of others.

Learning how to keep the armor on and how to use it to fight Satan is necessary if we are to continue maturing as children of God.

WINNING SPIRITUAL BATTLES

Even though I am a college professor with a great deal of formal education in my background, I can still feel quite intimidated whenever I visit a video arcade room at a shopping mall near my home. There are people of all ages, most of whom are much younger that I am, standing in front of various video machines busily depositing their quarters. It is quite an experience for me to walk around the arcade trying to figure out exactly what it is the various participants are attempting to accomplish. It is amazing to watch even some of the smallest children demonstrate their concentration and dexterity while playing these games. I would by no means challenge any of them, as I would surely reveal my age as well as my lack of ability!

I can remember the first time I ventured inside an arcade. I felt a bit of wonder and awe at the intelligence of those who could design such machines, but the wonder quickly turned to a feeling of inadequacy as I realized that almost anyone in there might easily have beaten me at any of the games.

It is common for a new Christian to experience some of these same feelings soon after he has accepted Christ as Savior. The normal step is to join a local church and watch how the Christians there "play the game." He is surely filled with wonder and awe at some of what he sees. But I wonder if this amazement does not soon change into intimidation as he considers actually trying some of the "games" himself. So often we expect him to be able to pick up the cues for what to do by simply observing the rest of us play. It often becomes a jumbled, frustrating experience, however, when no one takes the time to explain how it all works.

Hopefully, some of the following examples will help you know how to be more effective in this matter of wearing the armor of God.

KEEPING THE *HELMET* ON STRAIGHT

When we accept Jesus as Lord and Savior of our lives, we are given "salvation." We do not have to worry about where we will spend eternity, but we do have to be concerned about our ability to be victorious over sin. Satan often throws a "dart of doubt" at us. Our helmet slips down over our eyes, and we are unable to see our proper relationship with the Father. At such a time we should reaffirm our trust in the Lord's ability to save and to keep us, and recall some verses in the Bible that provide assurance of our position with Christ.

Another way Satan tries to get past our helmets and into our minds to defeat us is to place an ugly or sinful thought in our minds and then accuse us of thinking it. We need to recognize his tactics and quickly replace his thoughts with a Bible verse or the words of a hymn. We also need to be cautious of the things we read and what we watch on television. He loves to place garbage into our minds through the use of the media, or even through the lips of a friend or acquaintance. Many spiritual battles are won or lost in the thought-life of the Christian. Care should be taken to see that our minds are always under the Lordship of Christ. Just as a car left in neutral can roll into a ditch, our minds, if left unattended, can wander off into evil thoughts and imaginings.

IS YOUR *BREASTPLATE* ON RIGHT?

In addition to the battleground of the Christian's mind, Satan attacks us in the area of our feelings. Since we are creatures of our emotions, he knows that if he can defeat us there he has probably succeeded in keeping us from many victories. He loves to discourage or depress the child of God. He is the great accuser and the great deceiver (Rev. 12:9–10). If our lives are not being lived in righteousness—for example, our confession for sins and our apologies kept up to date—he is able to get past the breastplate and stab us in the heart with a negative emotion.

It is imperative that the quality of holiness characterizes our entire being. If any portion of our lives is not under the Lordship of Christ, Satan has a roadway into all other portions. A regular time of spiritual reflection and inventory is necessary to detect if any sin has gone unconfessed or any portion of our lives is not pleasing to Him.

IS THE *BELT* ON TIGHT?

In this world of white lies, cheating on taxes, and other compromises of the truth, it is often difficult for the Christian to refrain from being a part of the world system. I realized this in particular one day when I received too much change from a stamp machine outside the post office. The next morning when the post office opened, I returned the money and explained to the clerk what had happened. He thanked me and remarked that many people had complained about losing their money, but that I was the first who had brought any back.

I would like to think that the machine had never made a mistake in the past. But I have seen the same reaction the postal clerk expressed when I have mentioned to a department store clerk or cashier at a restaurant that I had been given too much change. Apparently, there is not much emphasis on honesty. Even large businesses report thousands of dollars in losses each year due to thefts by their own employees. If our "belts" are to be tight, we need to be living, speaking and dealing honestly in all areas of our lives.

HOW IS YOUR *SHIELD*?

In a commercial of many years ago, Colgate was trying to demonstrate the ability of its toothpaste to guard teeth from decay. The "guard-all shield" was around the person, and nothing harmful could get through. For Christians, the spiritual guard-all shield is faith. If our faith is small, the evil one can successfully throw at us all kinds of fiery darts that will hinder our progress in the spiritual life.

Jesus taught that it takes only faith the size of a mustard seed to be able to accomplish great things. If we discover that our faith is too small, however, what can we do? Just wishing we had more is not enough.

Basically, our faith grows in five ways:

1. As a result of a vital union with the Holy Spirit (Gal. 5:22–23). As we are filled with the Spirit, we will be filled with this portion of fruit. (See Chapter Six for a discussion on this subject.)

2. As we read and study God's Word (Rom. 10:17). By learning what God has promised to us, it is easier to trust Him to keep these promises. By reading and rereading what He says He will do for us, we are finally able to believe Him and act upon these promises.

3. By asking the Lord to increase our faith (Lk. 17:5). When we arrive at the place where we realize He is the only one who can grant us the faith that we need, we are then at the place to ask and to receive from Him.

4. As we spend time in prayer (Jude 20).

Nothing seems to help the life of faith more than praying and watching the Lord work. Just as we learn to ride a bicycle by getting on it and practicing, so we must spend time in prayer, actually exercising our faith muscles.

5. Through times of trial and testing (1 Pet. 1:6–7). Although we may prefer some of the other ways that faith grows, it is important to realize that some of the best lessons of faith are learned in the valleys of life. The insect in the cocoon will never be a beautiful butterfly without the struggle to be free. God often withholds His help until we have struggled enough to develop some faith-muscle He is working on.

DO YOU HAVE YOUR SHOES ON?

A few years ago I was able to visit Jerusalem and to go into the Moslem mosque that is presently on the site where Herod's temple once stood. Before we were allowed to enter the mosque, we were required to remove our shoes. When we were finished with our visit, we found our shoes, put them on, and went on our way.

In Palestine, in the days of Jesus, a person would remove his dusty sandals before entering the home. A servant, if the family had one, would wash the dirt from his feet, and he would enter the house barefoot. Whenever he put his sandals back on, it would signify that he was about to go out again.

A Christian who has his spiritual shoes on is obviously on the move spiritually. He is growing as a Christian and is engaged in rescuing others out of the grip of Satan. He knows how to lead a person to accept Christ as Savior (See Chapter Seven for more information) and is neither AWOL from his "regiment" nor inactively sitting on the sidelines watching others do all of the fighting.

USING YOUR *OFFENSIVE* WEAPON

All of us have undoubtedly watched a fight scene in a movie in which one of the persons, wielding a stick or sword, was frantically chasing an intended victim. The person without a weapon had to rely upon flight or some other evasive action to avoid being overcome by his opponent. At some point, however, the hero in the scene was able to obtain an advantage over the attacker by grabbing a plank or other weapon, at which time he clobbered the villain. We were relieved as our hero won the contest just in time for the show's last commercial to be shown.

Television fight scenes may entertain us, but they can also give us valuable insights into some of the battles with Satan in which we are engaged. One of the most obvious lessons is that we will have to run from the attacker only if we do not have our own offensive weapon ready. In the thick of the battle is not the time to be looking for our weapon or to be loading it. Preparation must be made before the confrontation.

God's Word must be studied and committed

to memory so that it will be available when attacks of Satan occur. In the heat of temptation and other times of struggle with the evil one, the Word of God must be so entrenched in our minds and hearts that God's Spirit in us can help us use it against Satan. (See Chapter One for more information on Bible study.)

ARE YOU *BREATHING?*

On a recent trip to Gatlinburg, Tennessee, I visited the famous Christus Gardens, a museum depicting the life of Christ in scenes using wax figures. It is quite an inspiring experience to view the dioramas and hear the taped music and narration of significant events in the biblical story. It is amazing how lifelike many of the wax figures appear. The real human hair and the vivid though artificial eyes that appear to be looking at you cause you to wonder at times if there are not some live characters intermingled with the wax ones. The best way to tell, of course, is to carefully check to see if the models are breathing. None of them were, so I had to conclude they were all wax figures!

Breath is an absolute essential for human life. Unfortunately, some professing Christians merely look as if they are alive. They are noticeably placed in strategic positions in the church, classroom or pew, so they appear to be genuine. But the real test is whether or not they are breathing. A Christian without a

strong prayer life will not be any more effective in his walk with the Lord or his struggles
with Satan than would one of the Christus
Gardens wax figures. (See Chapter Two for
more discussion on prayer.)

As long as Satan can deceive the believer
into thinking that he does not exist or that the
spiritual warfare is not really serious, he will
have succeeded in keeping him from maturing
as he should. Growth as a Christian must
include an understanding of the seriousness
of the spiritual warfare that is taking place, a
knowledge of how to appropriate the armor of
God, and a willingness to enter the battle itself.

Attention, Christian! Are you truly desirous
of spiritual growth, so that you may be an
effective soldier in Christ's army? Then you
must stand firm, as your King has commanded, against the schemes of the devil. Always remember that our real struggle is "not
against flesh and blood, but against the rul-
ers, against the powers, against the world
forces of this darkness. . . ."

Are you ready to rise to the challenge? Take
up the full armor of God and be strong in the
Lord!

HOW PREPARED ARE YOU?

Spiritual Armor	DOING GREAT	DOING OKAY	BELOW PAR	LITTLE/ NONE
1. Power over sin				
2. Righteous living				
3. Honesty, steadfastness				
4. Faith				
5. Witnessing to others				
6. Using God's Word				
7. Prayer				

Specific plans to help my spiritual growth:

Notes

CHAPTER FIVE

USEFULNESS IN MINISTRY

You may have wondered, as have I, why the Lord did not take us home to be with Him in heaven the moment we became His children. You also may have wondered how you could express your appreciation to Him for rescuing you from your sins and giving you the honor of being called His child. The answer to both, at least in part, seems to be in understanding the concept of spiritual gifts and how we are to be utilizing the one or more the Lord has given us.

When we became His children, we were placed into a brotherhood of redeemed individuals called in Scripture "the body of Christ." We were given a gift or gifts at that time, as part of that body whose primary job is to accomplish the work of the Lord in the world. Since He is no longer here in bodily form, His work is now accomplished through His spiritual body, the Church. The work is always the same: to reach the lost and to help Christians grow in their walk with the Lord.

In order for us to continue growing in the Christian life and be truly useful in ministry, it is necessary for us to be certain we understand what spiritual gifts are and that we find and use ours as effectively as possible.

BASIC PRINCIPLES CONCERNING
SPIRITUAL GIFTS

There are four passages in Scripture which are especially helpful as we seek to understand God's basic principles regarding spiritual gifts. The most used passage is 1 Corinthians 12. Let us analyze this chapter.

1. Spiritual gifts are described as special endowments of supernatural power, not inherited talents. They are given to the believer by the Holy Spirit. Of course, the Lord expects us also to use our inherited talents in His service. Many times the spiritual gifts the Lord gives us will complement our talents, but this is not necessarily the case.

The pastor of my home church inherited a beautiful singing voice and the ability to play the piano "by ear." He majored in music in college, thinking that the Lord wanted him to be a minister of music. While in seminary, however, the Lord called him to preach, indicating to him that his spiritual gift was preaching. He will sometimes sing a song during one of his sermons, so he is still using his musical abilities for the Lord, but his primary ministry involves his spiritual gift of effective preaching.

2. The Lord does not want us to be misinformed about the gifts and the particular ones He has given to us (v. 1). Many Christians do

not utilize their gifts because they have never been made aware of them or how to use them.

I led a study at my present church on how to discover your spiritual gifts. What a blessing it was to help people find and use their spiritual gifts!

3. This passage also teaches us that there are diversities of gifts (v. 4). Christians are not expected to have all of the gifts. The gifts vary widely, and some may be more valuable than others, but none is unimportant. They are given by the same Spirit, in order to serve the same Lord, and are inspired by the same God (vs. 4–6). No one should feel inferior if the gift he has received seems not to be as important as the one someone else has been given. The "body of Christ" can only function properly if everyone is using the gift given to him (vs. 14–26).

4. Each born-again believer has been given at least one spiritual gift, which the Lord expects him to exercise for the welfare of the whole body of believers (v. 7). Some Christians seem to have multiple gifts, but all of us can be assured that we have received at least one gift that the Lord expects us to use.

5. The Holy Spirit apportions the gifts as He desires (v. 11). All are gifts of grace. It is by His wisdom, not according to our merit, that we are given specific gifts. As we come to understand this truth, it will protect us both from pride and a sense of inferiority. How can we brag because we have a certain gift *or* feel less spiritual than someone else if we understand

that our gifts are not determined by our own abilities or lack of them?

6. Each of us needs to utilize our gifts for the benefit of the other members of the body. If any of us are not using our gifts, then all the rest are missing out in some way. None of us can progress as we should in spiritual growth unless each member of the body is functioning properly (vs. 20–22).

7. If we are eager for certain gifts, we need to seek the ones that especially build up the body of Christ. We should not be selfish and desire the ones that we think will benefit us personally. The purpose of spiritual gifts is for the spiritual growth and maturity of the entire body of believers, not for an individual's own edification (v. 27).

8. We are exhorted to desire the greater gifts (v. 31) while exercising the gifts we already have, but it is important to keep in mind that more valuable than any spiritual gift is *love* (Greek: *agape*). If we had all the spiritual gifts and did not have this divine type of love, they would be useless.

ADDITIONAL PRINCIPLES

There are three passages in the New Testament in which are set forth three other important principles to aid us in our understanding concerning spiritual gifts: 1 Timothy 4:14; Romans 11:29; and Ephesians 4:11–14.

1. We should not neglect the gift that is in us. God expects us to use our gifts. But first it

is necessary for us to discover what our gifts are before we can utilize them properly.

2. God's gifts are irrevocable; He never withdraws them. Many times we can lose the benefit of a talent by failing to use it. With God's gifts, however, whenever we decide to use them, His Spirit is there to empower us.

3. Gifts have been given for a specific reason. Their purpose is to perfect and equip Christians to minister to each other until all come to Christian maturity. Until each Christian discovers and uses his spiritual gift or gifts, the body of Christ will remain immature.

A LOOK AT THE GIFTS THEMSELVES

There are three key passages in the Bible which will help us as we try to determine what are the spiritual gifts the Lord has given to His body: 1 Corinthians 12; Romans 12; and Ephesians 4. Some of these gifts are expressed as functions; others are given as descriptions of individuals who have specific ministries within the church. (These definitions are taken from: *The Daily Bible Study Commentaries*, Wm. Barclay, Westminster Press; *Discovering Your Spiritual Gifts, Training Module*, Baptist Sunday School Board; and *The Gifts of the Spirit*, Jack McGorman, Broadman/Holman.)

INDIVIDUAL GIFTS

Word of Wisdom: The ability to understand the mind of God and His purposes and to share this with other Christians. This is a spiritual insight into the deeper truths of the faith—into theological teachings that are not obvious to all Christians. This gift may perhaps be evidenced in a deeply spiritual professor, a theologian, or a pastor. This gift would be especially valuable in a foreign mission situation. Paul himself had this gift (1 Cor. 2:6).

Word of Knowledge: The ability to give God's viewpoint on any given situation and to impart it to individuals or groups concerned. This is the gift that enables its recipient to help other people grasp spiritual teachings in clearly understandable terms. A person who has this gift is able to get to the heart of a problem and apply God's truths to it. (Paul exercised this gift throughout his epistles.)

Faith: This is a special kind of wonder-working faith, the kind that is described in the Bible as being able to move mountains. This in not the faith which all Christians are supposed to exercise, but a special kind of gift that God gives to some of His children in order that they may accomplish the miraculous. An example of this is God's use of George Müeller to build and maintain an orphanage when there was no human way this task could be accomplished.

Gifts of Healing: The ability to supernaturally impart God's healing to the physical or emotional needs of someone. As spoken of in Scripture, this gift is something above and beyond the normal abilities which are exercised by those in the medical profession. Christian doctors, nurses, psychologists and counselors who have this gift can exercise it along with their natural abilities and training. God uses prayer and the laying on of hands by those who have this gift as a way to heal the various illnesses of His children when normal means have failed or are not available.

Working of Miracles: This includes exorcism—the casting out of evil spirits—as in Acts 16:16–18. It also embraces the miraculous, instant healing of an incurable mental or physical condition—and other wonders, like the blinding of Elymas in Acts 13:8–11.

Discerning of Spirits: The ability to distinguish between spiritual reality and its counterfeits—what is of God and what is of Satan (See 1 John 4:1). A person who has this gift is able to attend a revival service and tell if the emotional enthusiasm present is from the Holy Spirit, is the work of deceiving spirits, or is merely human hysteria. He will be able to discern whether an individual is mentally ill or demon possessed.

Tongues: Speaking in a language that has not been learned by the speaker. It may be an intelligible language or the heavenly language that requires an interpretation. This gift may be given for public or private use.

Interpretation of Tongues: The ability to interpret the utterances of someone who has the gift of tongues, in order that the hearers may benefit.

All of the above are gifts given to individuals

for the corporate benefit of the body of Christ. They are listed in 1 Corinthians 12.

The next set of gifts are given to people as specific tools for the creation or building up of the church. These are listed in Ephesians 4 and Romans 12, as well as in 1 Corinthians 12:28.

Apostles: Itinerant church planters who have widespread authority over groups of churches.

Prophets: Those with the gift of preaching and exhorting: namely, the forth-telling of the Word of God. Some fore-telling of future events may be involved, but primarily the prophet's role is to give advice and guidance in addition to rebuke and warning from the Lord.

Administrators: Those who have organizational gifts, who enable the church and its various ministries to function effectively. Such a person often works behind the scenes to plan and organize the work of the church so that it may run as efficiently as possible. Many Ministers of Education, Business Managers, and committee chairpersons could fall into this category.

Evangelists: Traveling preachers whom God uses to reach the unsaved. They do not have the widespread authority of the prophets or apostles.

Pastor–Teachers: Those who are settled and permanent in the upbuilding of one congregation, who shepherd and care for the church members and teach and nurture new converts.

Teachers: Those who build up people in the

faith—imparting to the church the doctrines of the faith in an understandable way.

Service: Showing the love of Christ in deeds of service to others. It is obvious, of course, that all Christians are to show kindness to others, but the person who has this gift is blessed by God in a different way as he serves others. A card to a shut-in or a hospital patient, a cake taken to a family in bereavement, a visit to a prison, or a meal for a homeless person could be some of the ways the Lord utilizes this gift in His children.

Exhortation: The ministry of encouraging and challenging. This can be the bringing of a public or private word of rebuke, challenge or encouragement. Some Christians have the God-given ability to make others feel better by sharing just the right word of encouragement, a smile, or a hearty handshake. Whether it is the youth worker who helps and encourages all the teenagers in Sunday School, or the usher at the door who welcomes visitors and members with a big smile and a cheery hello, God has blessed us by placing the people with this gift among us.

Contributing: Sharing our financial resources with those who are less fortunate. The Lord expects all of us to be cheerful givers and to be faithful in giving to Him our tithes and offerings. He has gifted some of His children, however, with the ability to bless others with their financial resources in a special way. The person does not have to have a lot of money, but that which he does have is used by God to impart a special blessing to someone without making him or her feel obligated.

Ruling: Occupying a position of leadership in the church and serving with enthusiasm and zeal. Many Christians hold leadership positions in the church, but the person with this spiritual gift adds the dimension of God-given ability to his or her service. It is this zeal for ministry that inspires others to serve and give of their best in the Lord's service.

Acts of Mercy: Lifting people up out of their sins and waywardness; reaching and helping those that others may have decided were hopeless cases. It is the ability to work with the "down and outs" that society has cast aside. It is the gift of being able to forgive those who have fallen into destructive sins in such a way that it restores them to wholeness once again.

Helpers: Those who have a particular ministry to those in need. God has a special place in His heart for those who cannot help themselves. He has gifted some of His children with the ability to be a blessing to these "special people." Whether it is serving as a visitor to the elderly homebound members of a congregation, or helping a widow cut her grass, "helpers," though often overlooked, are a tremendous blessing to the body of Christ.

LET'S BE PRACTICAL

These gifts are distributed by the Holy Spirit to the body of Christ for the benefit of the whole church. As a result, we can be confident that God will reveal the possession of these gifts not only to the individual concerned but to the leadership and members of the fellowship among whom He has placed these people. We need to bear in mind that these gifts are never given for the exaltation of the individual.

GUIDELINES FOR FINDING YOUR SPIRITUAL GIFT

It is possible for a person to make a special effort to discover what his spiritual gift is, yet not be able to find it. One of the causes for this may be the fact that one or more of the guidelines has not been met. God is not playing a hide-and-seek game with us concerning the gifts; He is very eager for us to know what they are and for us to use them in His kingdom's work. Anyone who makes a serious study in this area and meets the guidelines will surely be shown by the Lord what is expected of him.

1. The person must be a Christian. One of the reasons some church members fail to discover and use their spiritual gifts is that they do not *have* any, for they have not been truly born again.

2. The Christian must be spiritual, not dwelling in the carnal state. A believer must enthrone Jesus as Lord of his life before he can discover his gifts and understand how to use them properly.

3. The seeker must have a willingness to

use the gift before God will reveal it to him. We cannot have the attitude: "Show me my gift and *then* I will decide whether or not I will use it."

4. The inquiring one must be an active member of a local congregation. Christians cannot grow and serve in isolation. God's gifts are designed for use in the body of Christ, so most of the gifts will find expression within local bodies or congregations of believers. Sometimes, however, they may best be exercised at your place of work. It is important to realize that the usage of your gift or gifts may change depending on the needs of the congregation of which you are a member or because of changes within the vocation in which the Lord has placed you.

DISCOVERING YOUR SPIRITUAL GIFT

After you have come to a basic understanding of the principles concerning spiritual gifts and what the gifts are, you are ready to begin to find yours. The first thing to do is answer the following questions as completely as possible:

1. If you could do anything to improve your church, what would you do?

2. If you could be assured of the Lord's leading, what position in the church would you fill or what ministry would you like to engage in?

3. What are some of your hobbies, or things that you really enjoy doing whenever you have a chance?

4. With what age-groups do you enjoy working?

5. What spiritual abilities have others said they feel you possess? Do others express appreciation for one ministry you have rather than another? Are you asked to do some things in the church more than other things?

6. If you could have any of the gifts you wanted, which would you choose? Why? How would you use them?

After you have answered these questions, spend some time in prayer, and then use the following principles to help you in your discovery. Please keep in mind that sometimes it takes a while before our gifts are confirmed. Don't give up the search until you are confident you have discovered at least one of your gifts. Sometimes the Lord does not reveal everything to us at once.

1. What gift or gifts did you say you would like to have? Often the desires and aspirations we have are caused by the gift that is in us wanting to be activated. What are some of the concerns for your church? What jobs would you like to hold in your church if you could be sure God wanted you there? Many people feel as if something could not possibly be a spiritual gift because they enjoy it so much. That is far from the truth. The fact that we enjoy a certain ministry or job is a good indication that it could be the gift that God has placed within us.

2. Other members of the body of Christ can be very helpful in giving us direction concerning

our spiritual gifts. Talk with others. Ask what abilities they see in you that may indicate your spiritual gift. We need to ask the Lord to help us realize that there is no room for spiritual pride in the matter of gifts. We must attempt to overcome the embarrassment or pride we may feel when we discuss the gifts in relation to ourselves and others. If we have a gift, it is because the Lord gave it to us. It is not the result of our own merits or abilities.

3. Try exercising what you think your gift is. Volunteer for some job in the church. Begin ministering in the area of your interests and desires. Gifts are to be used, not to be collected as charms on a bracelet and worn to impress others.

4. Wait on the Lord. In the final analysis, the presence or absence of a gift will be confirmed over a time period. If your gift is genuine, and you are walking in the Spirit under the Lordship of Jesus, you will notice a few things. You will enjoy your ministry and will not feel burdened by the work. Visible results will occur. The Lord, however, may limit these to keep us from becoming puffed up with pride. We will be able to see enough results, however, to assure us we are on the right track.

Confirmation will come—not because we feel good about what we are doing but because lives will be changed or helped. God's gifts are to be used for the benefit of others in the body of Christ. As others are helped, we will receive the confirmation we need to prove to us that we are indeed using the spiritual gift that God has given to us.

RATE YOURSELF
Usefulness in Ministry

	YES	NO	UNSURE
1. Have you discovered your spiritual gifts?	☐	☐	☐
2. Are you effectively using your gifts?	☐	☐	☐
3. Are you consistently using your gifts?	☐	☐	☐
4. Are you seeing fruit from your ministry?	☐	☐	☐
5. Are you helping others find and use their spiritual gifts?	☐	☐	☐
6. Do you know of Christians who have gifts but don't seem to be using them?	☐	☐	☐
7. Have you noticed how the body of Christ suffers when you or someone else fails to use their spiritual gifts?	☐	☐	☐
8. Can you think of better ways to use your spiritual gift?	☐	☐	☐

Specific plans, suggestions or reminders:

CHAPTER SIX

CHECKING UP ON YOUR FRUIT-BEARING

Jesus taught His disciples that one of the indications of a true follower of the Lord is that he brings forth good fruit (Matt. 7:17–20). He declared that He specifically chose us to bring forth fruit (Jn. 15:16). God has created us to bring forth good works for His glory (Eph. 2:10). In fact, says the Scripture, such works serve as an evidence of one's faith and salvation (Jas. 2:14–18).

What kind of fruit, and how much, does the Lord expect of us? Is the fruit we are to bear manifested in behavior, in attitude, or both? Or does our fruit consist only of those individuals whom we have lead to Christ?

The Bible indicates that all of us are to be witnesses, and that some will be sowers, while others will reap (Acts 1:8; Jn. 4:34–38). But soul-winning, important as it is, is not essentially what Jesus meant when He spoke of our bearing fruit. The Holy Spirit entered our lives when we accepted Christ as Savior, and there is a connection between that event and our capability and responsibility to be fruit-bearers.

Galatians 5:22–23 informs us of the fruit

that the Holy Spirit's presence within us will produce: love, joy, peace, patience, gentleness, goodness, faith, meekness and self-control. It is quite easy to see that it is not something we can produce by our own efforts. Since Jesus has said that He expects to see this fruit in our lives, it will be helpful to come to a better understanding of how we may be more successful in this matter.

A LOOK AT THE FRUIT

The pieces of the fruit the Holy Spirit produces are listed in Galatians 5:22–23. (Basic definitions are taken from *The Letters to the Galatians and Ephesians*, Wm. Barclay, Westminster Press, 1958).

Love: True affection for God and man growing out of God's love for and in us. A careful study of 1 Corinthians 13 will reveal some of the specific ways God expects us to love Him and others. As we read this "love chapter," it becomes obvious that the qualities of love mentioned are divinely produced.

Joy: Gladness; delight which has its basis in Christian faith and whose real foundation is God. Happiness is dependent on circumstances; joy is dependent on our relationship with God. We can have joy even when circumstances have made us unhappy. It is deeper than the emotional feelings that change with the weather, our health, or our environment. It is the stability of knowing that God is in charge even when our world is falling apart.

Peace: This fruit reveals itself in many forms, which can be grouped together as follows: (a) Freedom from fears, agitating passions, and moral conflicts. When we have this inner peace, we will not be troubled with anxieties and fears. Our emotions will not be churning like the agitator in a washing machine. We will not be torn between what is right and what is wrong. (b) Assurance of salvation; not being afraid of God; being content with our earthly lot, whatever that is. A person who is afraid of what God will do to him does not have peace. A person who allows the Spirit to produce the fruit of peace within him will know he is right with God and will be happy with the life that God has chosen for him.

Patience: Calm endurance without complaint. The patient person will be able to go through the trials and tests of life with the calm assurance that God is in control. When circumstances or people try his patience, he leans harder on the indwelling Spirit—who produces a calmness that helps him endure the problems without murmuring or complaining.

Gentleness: Kindness which does not rebuke, only helps. The story is told of a man who had a can of oil that he took everywhere with him. Whenever he found a noisy door or a squeaky hinge, he would apply a few drops of oil to it. Although considered eccentric by many, he felt he could make his world a better place by eliminating some of the environmental harshness. This fruit of the Spirit, gentleness, is a lot like that can of oil. It looks for opportunities to alleviate the noise and harshness in a life by adding a kind word or deed, the oil of a gentle spirit.

Goodness: An uprightness of soul which causes one to reach out to others to do good even when it is not deserved. But it can also rebuke and discipline: goodness is the righteous indignation that Jesus expressed when He chased the moneychangers out of the temple because they were desecrating it and cheating the people. In short, goodness is concerned with the injustices in life, even if it means expressing anger at injustice. The anger, however, must be directed at the deed, not at the person. The Holy Spirit can give us guidance to know when our anger is justified.

Faith: The leaning of the entire personality on God in absolute trust and confidence in His power, wisdom, and goodness. The ability to trust God with our lives and with all that concerns us comes from having this fruit produced in our lives by the Spirit. The ability to trust God is not some effort of mental self-persuasion but is a natural result of relying upon the Spirit who dwells within us. Jesus is Himself both the author and finisher of our faith (Heb. 12:2).

Another translation of the Greek word *pistis* is "faithfulness" or "fidelity." (Most modern Bible versions translate it so here.) Faithfulness is the quality which renders a person trustworthy or reliable, like the faithful steward in Luke 12:42–48 and the two faithful servants in Luke 19:11–19. Its importance in God's eyes is revealed also in Revelation 2:9 and 17:14.

Meekness: This piece of fruit has three aspects to it. (a) Submissiveness to the will of God. (b) Teachableness; not being too proud to learn. (c) Consideration; thoughtfulness for others. If this fruit is manifested in our lives, we will have all three aspects. When we are submissive, we have a "Yes, Sir" attitude toward God; we are ready to do what He says when He says it. There should not be any question as to our obedience when we have received clarification as to what He wants us to do.

We should never feel as if we have learned all there is to know about our walk with the Lord. Many times He would teach us new lessons and insights if only we were more teachable. Because His lessons sometimes come through the most unlikely teachers, we should be watching for the messages He wants to give us.

Christians should be the most considerate people on the earth. Instead we often are very harsh and critical of those who disagree with us. If the Spirit is allowed freedom in our lives, He will produce a considerate spirit that will result in behavior that will glorify God and bless people.

Temperance: This is an older word for self-control. Basically it means that the "self" or old nature will be under the dominance of the Spirit if He is allowed to produce this fruit in our lives. (See Chapter Three for a discussion of the "self.")

These nine virtues are set in stark contrast to fifteen or more works of the old nature enumerated in verses 19–21. Only the Holy Spirit within the yielded life of a believer is able to produce such a lovely new-nature "bowl of fruit."

REASONS FOR FRUIT-BEARING

A genuine Christian will have a strong desire to bear good fruit. Some Christians appear to have the idea that once they are saved they can live their lives in whatever manner they wish—but this is a mistake.

Does the Bible shed any light on the reasons why we as Christians should be bearing spiritual fruit?

1. It brings glory to God (Matt. 5:16; Jn. 15:8; Phil. 1:11). A careful examination of the fruit of the Spirit in Galatians 5 will convince most people that the qualities listed there are not common to the experience of man. We may have some traits that are similarly named, but the genuine product obviously is foreign to man's nature. The qualities are placed in the heart of the believer by the Holy Spirit Himself. The fruit is so different from anything we can produce for ourselves that it results in bringing glory to the One who produces it. Christians and non-Christians alike are impressed with the life of one in whom these godly traits are being manifested. One result is a respect for the person who is yielded to God, but the ultimate response of the heart

is praise to the One who is gracious and powerful enough to reveal Himself through the life of a mere mortal.

2. We have been specifically selected by God to be fruit-bearers (Jn. 15:16; Eph. 2:10). God certainly could have ordained that angels be the vessels through whom He would reveal His attributes to the world. But in His great wisdom He decided that redeemed humanity would be the agency through which He would show His grace and love to the rest of mankind. We were saved to serve and to show the world what God can do with a life yielded to Him. A Christian who is not in the will of God in this matter of fruit-bearing is like a fish out of water. We were created to bear fruit.

And so the reason we were left on this earth after our own redemption is that we are to be fruit-bearers (Rom. 7:4). When Jesus came into our hearts and redeemed us, He made us fit for heaven. Theoretically, God could have translated us out of this realm and into another at the moment we invited Jesus into our lives. However, He designed us to be the body through whom He would continue His ministry on this earth (1 Cor. 12:27). He desires hearts through whom He may love, hands by which He may touch, lips through which He might speak. Our bodies are to be vessels for His use.

3. Fruit-bearing is one way to be pleasing to God (Col. 1:10). If a person has had a living experience with the Lord, there is a desire to express appreciation for what He has done.

There is an excitement to share the news of redemption with others, but there is also an earnest desire to let the Lord know how great it is to be rescued from the clutches of death and hell. Jesus Himself said that when we minister to others we are showing our love to Him (Matt. 25:40).

4. Fruit-bearing is a good way to let others know that we are Christians (Matt. 7:16–20). A term used by unbelievers to describe some Christians is "hypocrite." The obvious reason is that they expect the believer to be living out in his daily experience what he professes. When the fruit is not obvious to the unbeliever, or when the old nature is in control of the Christian's actions, the conclusion is reached that the person must be a hypocrite—a phony. William James, a well-known psychologist of a century ago, although not a professing Christian himself, seemed to have great insight into this matter of fruit-bearing. One of his conclusions, after studying the conversion experiences of many professing Christians, was summed up in a few words: "Fruit, not roots." What he obviously meant to convey to the Christian world was the fact that unbelievers are not so much interested in our impressive-sounding testimonies as they are in seeing fruit in our lives. They do not want to hear the pious phrases; they want to see love and patience and kindness and gentleness manifested in our relationships among ourselves and with them.

PRINCIPLES OF FRUIT-BEARING

Until I was invited to teach at a college located in a small town in North Carolina, I had always lived in a large city. When I moved to the rural area, I rented a farmhouse on seven acres of land in order to get a taste of how "the other half" lives. One of my first projects on the farm was to plant a garden. Naturally, I knew absolutely nothing about how to go about such an undertaking, so I relied heavily on the expertise and kindness of the neighbors. Some of you may think it strange that I did not know how deep to plant my seeds, in what position the potato eyes were to be placed, where to apply the fertilizer . . . and a whole long list of other procedures if one's garden is to be a success. Even though that first year I made many mistakes—such as pulling up the young okra plants and leaving a row of pokeweed growing, killing a whole bed of strawberries by adding fresh chicken manure to the young plants—I did learn, and now feel reasonably experienced in the matter of tending a garden.

I made just as many mistakes as a new Christian while attempting to learn how a young believer should grow in order to produce fruit. But through the loving guidance of more mature believers, I was able to learn the principles necessary for spiritual fruit-bearing in the garden of my life.

1. Only a good tree can bring forth good fruit (Matt. 7:15–20). I heard someone use the

illustration that "being a church member would not make a person a Christian any more than sitting in a garage would make someone a car." I know from the experiences of my own religious pilgrimage and that of many of my family members that it is all too easy to think one is a Christian just because he has been baptized or joined a church. And many unbelievers do try hard to manifest some of the attributes of spirituality in their lives. But genuine fruit will only be seen on a real tree. A profession of faith in Jesus is not enough; a relationship with Him through repentance and faith is what makes the tree genuine.

2. The condition of the soil affects the amount of fruit produced (Matt. 13:1–23). In the parable of the sower and the seed, Jesus revealed that the condition of the soil directly affects the ability of the seed to produce fruit. On hard ground, the seed cannot take root. On rocky soil, the roots will not be deep enough to allow the plant to survive the hot sun. And thorn-infested soil chokes out the plant. It is only the good soil that allows for adequate fruit-bearing.

We are the soil. If our hearts are hard, or our minds closed by stubbornness, the seed will not be accepted into the life. If we have but shallow commitment, our faith will not endure the trials that come our way. If our lives are caught up in the cares and concerns of this life, the fruit will be skimpy at best. The Lord desires that our lives be good soil, open to His sunshine, rain and pruning, so that the fruitfulness of the harvest will be great and will bring glory to His name.

3. The specifics of fruit-bearing will be different for each Christian (Jn. 4:35–38). The Lord desires that each of us should bear fruit according to our own abilities and gifts. Some are sowers, others are reapers. Some speak a word of witness, others stay at home and pray. Some plant the seeds of truth in a person's mind, and years later someone else has the joy of actually leading the person to faith in Christ.

Some are the ears of the body of Christ, others are His eyes. Some of us may be like a wildflower blooming atop an isolated mountain for only God to know about and enjoy. Others will bear fruit in a setting that will be obvious to the multitudes. Our responsibility is to be fruit-bearers. The specifics are left up to Him.

4. Our fruit-bearing is dependent on a vital relationship with the Lord Himself (Jn. 15:1–16). During the early years of my Christian experience I was determined to be a committed Christian and to do my best to have in my life the Christian qualities that are expected of believers. I would try to be loving to those who were unlovable. I would attempt to be patient toward those who were aggravating. I would struggle to be sweet to those who were being unkind to me. As you can surely guess, it wasn't long before I realized that this endeavor was futile! At times I would find some comfort in the fact that all of us are human, or I would pride myself on some progress in this area

when I noticed that others were not as successful as I. But in my heart I knew that what I was expecting was not possible in human strength. That is when I began to search and to discover the truths found in John 15.

Jesus is the only one who can produce the Christian life in us. In the power of the Holy Spirit, and in reliance on the written Word of God to keep us in contact with the living Word of God, we can be vessels in whom the attributes of the Spirit are manifested.

5. Discipline is necessary to make us more fruitful (Heb. 12:11). One evening during the summer when I was too sick to tend to my regular chore of mowing our extensive lawn, my sister offered to do the job for me. Since she was unfamiliar with how the riding lawn mower worked, I was a bit reluctant to accept her offer. Since the grass was nearly knee-high, however, I decided to let her give it a try. After giving her a quick lesson on how to run the mower, I went back into the house. I glanced out of the bedroom window occasionally to see if I needed to continue praying for her, the lawn mower, and the shrubs in the yard. She seemed to be getting along fine, so I fell asleep. When I awoke it had turned dark; I went into the other part of the house to see if she had come in. I was anxious to hear about her new experience and to be sure that she, the lawn mower, and the shrubs had survived.

When I questioned her as to how the evening went, she replied that everything had gone all right until it had become too dark to see. She was determined to finish, she reported, so for the last thirty minutes she had been "flying by instruments." She mentioned that she had encountered one little problem, but felt as if it would turn out all right. She related that she had run over what she thought were old broccoli plants left from the summer garden. She assured me, however, that the lawn mower had not been harmed.

I knew immediately that she had not cut down the old broccoli plants, as I had already cleaned those out of that part of the yard. Upon questioning her further, I realized that she had driven the lawn mower over the new rose bushes that I had planted along the edge of the yard! She mentioned that she had ridden over them backward and forward to make sure they were completely cut down!

I assumed that I would have to replace the rose bushes the following season, so I tried not to let the situation upset me. Much to my surprise the next spring, the rose bushes (which had been reduced to one-inch stubs) were growing beautifully and produced that summer some of the prettiest roses I have ever seen! What I thought had destroyed them had actually helped them produce. They had been pruned.

Discipline and pruning by the Lord often seem harsh and destructive. But the Lord knows that often His best fruit will be produced on the tree or vine that has been subjected to His pruning.

6. We never become too old to bear fruit (Ps. 92:13–15). I serve part-time as an education director in a local church. Each summer we ask the congregation to fill out a Christian Service Survey which indicates where they would be willing to serve during the following year. One morning I was distributing the survey forms in various Sunday School classes in an attempt to have wider participation. When I entered a senior adult ladies' class and announced what I wanted them to do, one of the ladies quickly replied, "Oh, those are for the young people to fill out." I turned to Psalm 92 in my Bible and asked her to read verses 13 through 15, and then I slipped out of the room to go to another class. I noticed later that the lady had completed one of the survey forms!

I wish I had such easy success with all of the senior adults in my church. It is easy to feel that because we have retired from our secular jobs, we should no longer be expected to fill any of the positions in the church. Nothing could be further from the truth. God expects us to use our spiritual gifts and to be fruit-bearing Christians as long as He gives us the strength to do so.

My niece works for a florist. On several occasions she has brought home from work the roses that have not sold and would not be fresh enough for sale the next day. We usually manage to find some sort of vase to put them in and take the opportunity to decorate our dinner table for the evening meal. Of course, the family always notices the roses and remarks about how pretty they are. Imagine, however, our reaction if one of the family members were to never mention the flowers but rather commented on the beauty of the vase. Surely, the rest of us would wonder why the vase was noticed and the roses ignored.

A similar phenomenon often occurs in this matter of fruit-bearing. Paul, in his second letter to the Corinthians (4:7), reminds his readers that they are simply to be the vessels in whom the Lord will dwell. Christians are to be the flower pots (earthen vessels) in whom the "Rose of Sharon" is to be manifested. If fruit-bearing is to be what God expects, the flowers will receive the attention and glory, not the clay pot.

HOW'S YOUR FRUIT-BEARING?

Fruit I'm Bearing	DOING GREAT	DOING OKAY	BELOW PAR	LITTLE/ NONE
1. Love				
2. Joy				
3. Peace				
4. Patience				
5. Gentleness				
6. Goodness				
7. Faith(fulness)				
8. Meekness				
9. Self-control				

Ways I can improve my fruit-bearing:

CHAPTER SEVEN

FULFILLING THE GREAT COMMISSION

It is obvious from a careful reading of the Gospels that one of the first evidences that someone had experienced a meaningful encounter with the Lord Jesus was the person's desire to tell others. The woman at the well in Samaria went into town to share with others what she had experienced in her encounter with the Messiah (Jn. 4:28–29). Two blind men were healed by Jesus and were warned not to tell anyone about it; instead, they "spread abroad His fame in all that country" (Matt. 9:30–31).

We too have heard jubilant testimonies. Jesus saves someone and the person's first reaction is to share the grand news with someone else. When a beggar finds bread, he wants to tell other beggars. When someone is cured of cancer, he wants to share the news with others who have this dreaded disease. When a blind man is made to see, his first concern seems to be for others who are blind. A true test of the genuineness of someone's experience with the Lord is his desire to share it with others.

Many have had the experience of being in the presence of a loved one during the last hours of his or her life. The desire to love and minister to the dying loved one often means listening to his last wishes or instructions about what he wants to have done after his death. Most of us would surely do our best to carry out the wishes of our loved one, even if it might mean hardship or personal sacrifice to us.

Just before Jesus ascended into heaven, He shared His "last wish" with His disciples. He commanded them to go and tell all nations the truth they had learned. Surely their desire was to carry out this special injunction of the Lord. And it seems obvious that if we are His disciples and have had a life-changing experience with Him, we too will want to carry out His greatest command.

PREPARATION FOR SHARING WITH OTHERS

Leading a person to accept Christ as Savior is a great privilege. It may be that not all of us will be so fortunate, but we all can bear witness to what He has done for us. Some Christians sow the seed, others reap the harvest. One of the best ways to be prepared to share with others is to look at our own salvation experience. As we learn to relate to others what Jesus has done for us, we will be taking the first step in becoming effective witnesses.

USING YOUR PERSONAL TESTIMONY

Organize your testimony around the following four areas:

1. What my life was like before I accepted Christ.
2. How I realized I needed Christ.
3. How I became a Christian.
4. How Christ helps me in my daily life.

Practice sharing your testimony with another Christian. Try to share the basic information in ten minutes or less. (You can always elaborate on any area about which the unconverted person may question you, but you don't want to lose him by being too detailed.) Be sure to ask the individual if he has ever experienced anything similar in his own life. And if he is showing an interest, be prepared to explain to him how he, too, can become a Christian.

HAVE A PLAN FOR SHARING THE GOSPEL

One of the problems many Christians mention as the reason they do not share their faith is that they do not know where to begin or what to say. They also express concern that someone may ask them a question that they cannot answer. Having a plan to go by in witnessing can help with each of these problems.

A specific plan can give a person confidence. A plan can free your mind of the stress of thinking about what you are going to say next. You are free to concentrate on what your prospect is saying and on praying for the Lord's presence in this witnessing encounter. You are more apt to control the conversation and therefore will probably stay on target better.

A plan can help you bring a person to a decision more quickly. It will also help you to keep from becoming confused. And as you share your faith in an orderly manner, it will help him develop confidence in what you are saying.

It is important for you to develop your own plan of witnessing. There are many different ones that you can study, but you need to design one that feels comfortable to you. By all means avoid sounding like you are giving a canned speech! Your approach should be natural and one that comes from the heart. An unbeliever will quickly detect whether you are motivated by a concern for him or whether you are simply trying to "add notches to your soul-winning belt."

As you share, be certain to avoid unnecessary tangents. Many lost people have pet peeves or theological debates they like to use to avoid discussing their own spiritual condition. Assure your listener of your interest in the topics he has mentioned, but tell him that you would like to discuss those issues after you deal with his basic relationship with the Savior.

Disregard any criticisms of the Bible. Don't spend time defending the Bible; have him read what it says, and tell him that you will discuss its reliability after he sees what it says. On most occasions, the Spirit of God will convict him as to its reliability as he reads it.

Try to distinguish between resistance to the message you are presenting and resentment. Be sensitive to God's Spirit at this point. Many a well-meaning Christian has continued to share the gospel with someone when he was not interested in hearing it. One approach to the problem is simply to ask the person if it is all right for you to show him a few Bible verses and to tell what Jesus means to you. Be certain to limit the occasion to this, and don't use the time to catch up on all of your talking for the week!

Be sensitive to expressions on the person's face and to his body language—such as folded arms, possibly indicating a closed point. Ask him if he understands the concept you have just shared.

If at all possible, try to talk to a person alone. If you are visiting with a family, have the partner you have taken along with you engage the others in conversation. There are occasions, however, when you can present your message to the whole family. Be certain to give each person the opportunity to ask any questions and to make a personal commitment to the Lord.

THE MESSAGE ITSELF

Just as you organized your personal testimony around the points mentioned above, any plan for sharing the gospel should be sure to include some basic facts of the gospel.

1. All persons are sinners in need of salvation (Rom. 3:23).
2. Sin exacts a terrible price: separation from God for all eternity (Rom. 6:23).
3. God provided a way for us to be saved by sending His Son to die on the cross for us (Jn. 3:16; Isa. 53:6).
4. A person must accept Jesus as Lord and Savior of his life by a personal act of faith (Jn. 1:12–13; Rom.10:9–10).

Various Scripture verses and illustrations may be selected as a way of presenting these concepts. Your Bible or New Testament should be marked so that you can turn easily to the verses you wish to use. I personally think it is best to use only one or two verses with each point so as not to confuse the prospect. Let him look at the verses as you point to them and read them out loud. Briefly explain the concept to him and move on to the next point.

Talk normally—in a calm, not preaching, tone of voice. Be in prayer as you talk, asking the Lord to bring him to the place of decision. After you have presented the gospel message, be sure to ask him if he would like to accept Jesus as his personal Lord and Savior. If he responds favorably, lead him in a prayer similar to the following:

Dear Lord, I confess that I am a sinner and I am sorry. Please forgive my sins. I open the door to my life and invite You to be my Lord and Savior. I ask You to help me to live for You from this moment on.

In Jesus' name I pray. Amen.

Talk with the new convert about the decision he has just made. Have him pray in his own words a prayer of thanks to the Lord for forgiving him and entering his life. (This is a good test to check the sincerity of the decision he has just made.) Encourage him to share this decision with someone he knows who would understand and be happy to learn of it. Explain to him the need to be involved in a local church in order to grow as a Christian. And be sure to follow up in a few days and begin discipling the young convert quickly, or make arrangements for someone else to do so.

SOME OTHER WAYS TO PRESENT THE GOSPEL MESSAGE

Some people who hear the challenge to witness to others may think that the only way this can be done is during house-to-house visitation, on a street corner outside a bar, or by an evangelist in a crusade meeting. In fact, there are as many ways to witness as there are individuals willing to do so. Each of us needs to discover the way that is comfortable for us. Consider some of the following ways as you try to discover one that will be comfortable to your own personality.

CULTIVATE A PROSPECT. Be a friend to a neighbor or co-worker. Develop a trust level so that when an opportunity to share your faith arises, the communication and trust will have already been established. In many of these situations, the friend or co-worker may ask you what makes your life happy, or why you have the strength to face a certain difficulty. At that point, of course, you must be prepared to offer him the gospel message.

INVITE SOMEONE TO CHURCH. One of the least threatening ways we can witness is to invite someone to attend our church. Most people do not overreact to such an invitation, and it is a good way to let people know of your concern and interest in them spiritually. Be sure to explain what your church has to offer to them, since some people have been affected negatively by a past experience with a church. Offer to give them a ride or take them out to dinner after the service. At some point you may be able to ask them if they would like a personal visit from the pastor or some other member of your church. An honest interest in people can go a long way in reaching them for the Lord.

TAKE ADVANTAGE OF MINISTRY OPPORTUNITIES. One of my aunts died last year. After the obituary appeared in the newspaper, I received a cordial letter from someone I did not know who expressed concern over the loss of my loved one. The writer assured me that the Lord was concerned about my loss, and that if I needed to talk with anyone who cared about me I could contact her or someone at a local Seventh Day Adventist Church. This experience made me wonder how many times we as the body of Christ overlook opportunities to reach people for the Lord when they may be the most reachable.

We should ask the Lord to show us ways we can reach out to the lost in ministry that may be the means of winning them to faith in Him. Of course, our ministry must not have the ulterior motive of getting members for our church. We should be genuinely concerned about the welfare of those who do not know Christ and should determine the best means to communicate this love and concern to them, even if they never join our church. Many a person has been led to know the Lord through the loving concern of a Christian who cared enough to give of himself to one going through a valley.

PARTICIPATE IN DOOR-TO-DOOR VISITATION. Some Christians will never feel comfortable going into the houses of people they do not know and trying to witness to them. There are others, however, who thoroughly enjoy the challenge of meeting people and who can enthusiastically give a witness to someone they have just met. Some Christians can accompany these "extroverts" on a visit and be the silent partner who prays while the other person is presenting the gospel.

USE A GOSPEL TRACT OR OTHER PIECE OF LITERATURE. One man who was a member in one of the churches where I served as Minister of Education always had a pocket full of tracts he would give out. He would give salvation tracts to non-Christians, and other materials that were appropriate for Christians. He would leave them in doctor's offices, bus stations, restaurants, and anywhere he felt that someone might pick them up and read them. He had found his own comfortable way of presenting a gospel witness.

There are many kinds of tracts, magazines and leaflets that are appropriate for such a ministry. One word of caution: Always read the material before you give it to someone. You need to be sure that the tract has been written in a tactful manner and is consistent with your theology. Although some "hell-fire and brimstone" approaches might be effective with some individuals, most people will probably respond more favorably to a message that shows them their need and the solution in such a way that it does not offend them.

On your latest trip to the shoe store you were probably made aware of the many different kinds of shoes available on the market today. You probably have wondered, as have I, if anyone actually wears some of the kinds that you see! Obviously the shoe manufacturing businesses have determined that there are different kinds of people with varying preferences in footwear. They are trying to meet these differences with their products.

We as witnesses for the Lord should also recognize the differences among people. In light of that, we should realize that Christians do not all have to present their witness to the world in the same way. We should try to determine under the leadership of the Lord what our basic approach should be and then be faithful to it. However, we should remember that unbelievers also respond differently to particular approaches. So don't be inflexible. A fisherman understands this principle. If the catfish bites better on bread or worms, it is futile to use shrimp, even though the bait is more sophisticated.

No one approach is more spiritual than another in the matter of being a fisher of men. God expects us to fulfill the Great Commission, whether it is by taking a cake to an unsaved neighbor who has lost a loved one and sympathetically showing heartfelt concern and Christian love, or by sitting down with an open Bible and systematically explaining the plan of salvation. Under the guidance and grace of God, commit yourself to wearing your "spiritual shoes" and to being faithful in this matter of presenting the gospel to those who are without Him. Jesus gave us an important task: to reach and teach the world about the grace and forgiveness available in a relationship with Him.

How are you doing in fulfilling the parting command of the Savior?

LOOKING AT MY LIFE

	YES	NO
1. I have shared my personal testimony with a lost person.	☐	☐
2. I have a plan I feel comfortable using to witness.	☐	☐
3. I have marked my Bible or a New Testament so I can easily share with a lost person.	☐	☐
4. I have discovered the most comfortable way for me to be a witness to the unsaved.	☐	☐
5. I pray regularly and specifically for the unsaved.	☐	☐

My plans for growth in sharing my faith with others:

CONCLUSION

My friend's brother ignored the signs that something might be wrong with his health. Eventually he reluctantly agreed to go to the doctor—and discovered that he had colon cancer. The most heartbreaking aspect of the story is that if he had gone in for treatment earlier, the outcome would have been much different.

A fellow choir member told me that her husband would not go to the doctor to find out why a sore on his finger would not heal— and now he is in the hospital receiving extensive chemotherapy treatments for acute leukemia.

There is much emphasis today on having regular checkups even when there are not any outward signs that something may be wrong. Insurance companies have been informed by the government that they now must pay for certain preventive exams and X-rays. Prevention has obviously been recognized as absolutely essential in our fight against cancer and other diseases.

But what about the Christian's regular checkups and prevention against the destructive disease of sin? Many of us make an effort to have our cholesterol level checked but overlook the matter of spiritual growth and development. We all too often fall into the trap of feeling that spiritual growth is an automatic result of growing older and attending church on a reasonably regular basis. We *hope* we are progressing in our relationship with the Lord, but we do not have any "scales" on which to be weighed or any "yardstick" to use as a measure.

It is my prayer and challenge that at least yearly you will use this book as an aid and determine to have a *regular checkup* in the most important area of your life . . . your walk with the Lord.

————

This book was produced by the Christian Literature Crusade. We hope it has been helpful to you in living the Christian life. CLC is a literature mission with ministry in over 45 countries worldwide. If you would like to know more about us, or are interested in opportunities to serve with a faith mission, we invite you to write to:

Christian Literature Crusade
P.O. Box 1449
Fort Washington, PA 19034